Parrot
Guide

by Cyril H. Rogers

A room devoted to breeding masked lovebirds in a California aviary. Photo by L. van der Meid.

Two peach-faced lovebirds "kissing" each other. Photo by Dr. M. M. Vriends.

Lovebirds in breeding cage. Photos by G. S. Axelrod.

Contents

A visit to the aviary of a zoo can offer one the opportunity to observe the behavior and temperament of cockatoos, such as these Moluccans. Photo by Dr. H. R. Axelrod.

Opposite: When the crest of a cockatoo is erected, a set of very colorful feathers is exposed, as seen in this citron-crested cockatoo. Photo courtesy of San Diego Zoo.

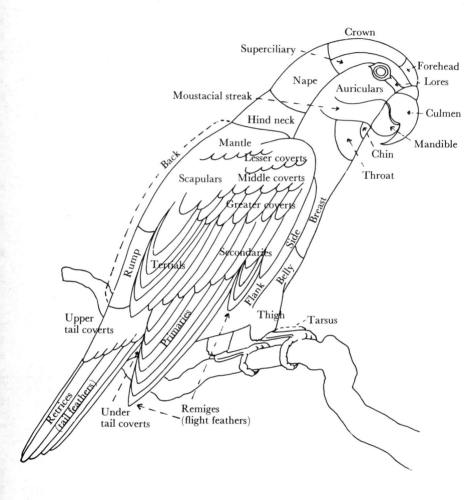

The terms used to describe the plumage and various parts of a bird. These terms are used for all species of birds, not just for parrots.

Parrots are family fun. Photo by T. Caravaglia.

Part I   The Parrot in the Home

1   Parrots are Fun

Over 100 years ago—1874, to be exact—a book on birds was publish-
ed in England. Its title was *Birds: Their Cages and Their Keep.* The
author, K.A. Buist, opened his book saying:

> A merciful man is merciful to his beast, why not to his
> birds? Reader, use your common sense, think of your
> feathered pets as you do your dog or horse, namely as a
> created, sensitive being, with a body to suffer, feelings to
> hurt, and frequently, brains to appreciate his condition, and
> you cannot go very far wrong in your treatment of him.

Up goes the rocket, with the passenger hanging outside. Photo courtesy of Parrot Jungle, Florida.

Parrots, even the small ones, are remarkably hardy creatures. Properly kept and fed, they will tolerate continual handling and still live to a ripe old age. Photo by T. Caravaglia.

Bathing is a regular activity of lovebirds. Their motions while bathing are sometimes comical. Photo by Dr. H. R. Axelrod.

A pair of the smaller parrots, such as these tuis, is a never-ending source of interest and delight. Photo by T. Caravaglia.

Author Buist had a great many more pertinent things to say about cage birds and their care, just as applicable today as they were then, but these few words summed up the essence of successful parrot keeping so fully that I could not refrain from beginning my book as Buist did his.

Common sense is his keyword. Empathy is mine. For the benefit of my younger readers, let me explain that that means identifying with the bird—putting yourself inside the parrot and seeing and feeling things from its bird's eye view.

Now, let me begin by saying that parrots, in their infinite variety, are the most beautiful of all birds. They are also, I must admit, noisy, but when we remember that their "noise" can transform itself into a mimicry of human speech and song, we are quite willing to overlook this minor fault. How captivating they are! How they conjure up the romantic past! Is there one among us who will ever forget "Cap'n Flint," the parrot in *Treasure Island,* and his constant squawk of "Pieces of eight . . . pieces of eight!" Or the parrot who voyaged on the raft *Kon Tiki* and spoke Spanish with a Norwegian accent?

Unlike the more usual pets, parrots bring their keepers the rewarding satisfaction of living close to the world of nature, and a savage world it is at that. Most of them come to us from tropical jungles, and how they conjure up those exotic foreign lands: the hills of India, the rice fields of Java, the bush country of Australia, the lush rain forests of the Amazon and the Equator and the jewel-like islands of the South Seas. All these are brought vividly into our lives by these swinging, winging, talking flashes of psychedelic color. As a matter of fact, they have so much and such variegated color that many people can look at a parrot for the first time and murmur, "There ain't no such bird!" The German authority J.M. Bechstein points out that their plumage may by some

> . . . be thought gaudy and too violently and abruptly contrasted, still we think no one can look at some of these gorgeously decked macaws, and splendid and effulgent lories, or the diversely tinted Australian parakeets without acknowledging them to be among the most beautiful and striking of the feathered race.

Turning to the more practical side, parrots are pleasing pets to keep. No other family of birds can approach them in their blend of beauty, tameness, intelligence and, as I have said, their amazing ability to imitate the human voice. They are highly sociable creatures. Like dogs and cats, they *like* living with man. They have been known to fall in love with their keepers and to pine away when separated from them. They make especially fine pets for lonely people. As one fancier puts it:

No other family of birds can approach the parrot in its blend of beauty, tameness and intelligence. Photo by Herrlich, Hamburg.

"Once a parrot has given you its heart, it will render you a touching and faithful devotion for the rest of your two lives." He also adds that such affection must be returned and that this can best be done by giving your pet plenty of companionship, by letting it out of its cage regularly—or by joining it in the aviary—and by seeing that it never, not ever, becomes bored.

A properly maintained parrot is clean, free from unpleasant odor, tamable and easily housed. Correctly cared for, the larger species have been known to live for fifty years, and some of them live much longer. Tales, however, that they live to be a hundred are usually discounted.

Some parrots I have known—African greys and South American amazons—have been in the same family for three generations. One particular African grey, Harry by name, lived with the same family for some 40 years and then suddenly laid two eggs. The owners found this hard to believe since for 40 years they had thought "he" was a male.

Even small parrots like the golden-wing will, with persistence, patience and love, learn to talk.

Opposite, top: Blue-fronted amazon, far from its jungle home. Photo by T. Caravaglia. Opposite, bottom: Anatomically and physiologically the largest macaw is similar to these golden-winged parrots. Photo by A. van den Nieuwenhuizen.

Harry lived nearly 20 years longer without producing another egg. Perhaps I should point out here that a tame pet hen may suddenly lay an odd egg or two without coming into contact with a male.

Some hypersensitive people feel that it is wrong to take a wild bird from the tropical jungle and cage it in our northern climes. On this subject we can only quote the authority Lee S. Crandall, at one time Curator of Birds at the New York Zoological Garden:

> The brain of a bird is not developed to the point which has been reached by the higher mammals. Even they become perfectly contented in captivity when properly housed, so why should not the bird? There are no grounds for believing that the avian mind is concerned with matters other than those of its daily existence. No one who has had personal experience with properly fed, correctly caged wild birds can doubt their contentment. Relieved from the problems of securing daily food, freed from the ever present dangers which throng their feral lives, their lot certainly is not that of the oppressed.

An African grey parrot. Photo by G. S. Axelrod.

Parrots, like most birds, prefer to perch on the highest vantage point from which they survey their domain. This parrot undoubtedly would prefer, if permitted, to perch on the man's head.

Just What Is a Parrot?

To most people a parrot is a thick-bodied, short-legged green bird with a large hooked bill and a fairly short but stubby tail. And they are right. This *is* a parrot, but then so is the familiar little grass parakeet (known also as the budgerigar) a parrot, and so are the great blue and gold or red and green macaws so familiar to visitors at zoos, and so are the great snowy cockatoos with their elaborate erectile crests. Yes, all of these are parrots, as are the more than 300 other members of the family. You may well then ask again: "What is a parrot?" Popularly the name parrot is used to specify the various green amazon parrots of South America and the grey parrots of Africa. However, any member of the bird family Psittacidae, which is in the order of Psittaciformes, whether it be a cockatoo, macaw, lory, lorikeet, conure, parrotlet, caique, lovebird or cockatiel is equally entitled to be called a parrot, and in this book we sometimes do just that. To avoid the constant qualifications of "parrot-type" or "parrot-like bird" which sprinkle the pages of more learned works, I use the word "parrot" whenever I generalize. When I am discussing a particular subfamily or species, I use its common and scientific name, but when I refer to the members of the Psittacidae in

21

A performing greater sulphur-crested cockatoo rides a bicycle along a tightrope.

Success! This blue and gold macaw has just pulled up the bucket and will receive his reward in the form of food within. Photo courtesy of Parrot Jungle, Florida.

Scarlet macaw and sulphur-crested cockatoo in an outdoor aviary. Photo by R. Hanson.

general, lumping over 300 species together, I call them parrots—plain and simple. I hope this is acceptable and that no reader will take me to task when I include the tiny lovebirds among the parrots.

One thing the parrots do have in common is their large, hooked bill which is similar to the beaks of the raptors or birds of prey, from which they may be distinguished by the following: the upper bill of the raptors (hawks, eagles, and owls) is solidly fused to the bones of the skull, while the upper mandible of the parrots is jointed and movable. In addition to this unique characteristic, parrots are zygodactyl—this means they have four toes on each foot; the outer two point forward, the inner two back, and these they use adeptly when climbing and conveying objects to their mouths. In climbing they also assist themselves with their remarkable beak, which is often used as a third foot.

Both the feet and the bill are extremely powerful; in fact, the bill of some species is capable of cracking the shells of nuts as hard as the Brazil nut. The tongue of the parrots is also unusual in that it is cylinder-shaped and thicker at the tip. With this tongue the parrot deftly extracts the meat from nuts or seeds as he cracks them.

As will be seen from our illustrations, not all parrots are green or even mainly green. They come in every color of the rainbow, both solid and varicolored. They come in various proportions and sizes, broad-winged, pointed-winged, long-tailed, short-tailed, rounded tails and pointed tails. Not all of them eat grains and seeds—many of them subsist on fruits and nectar—but once again, they all have in common the characteristic hinged beak, fleshy tongue and powerful four-toed feet.

THE GROUPINGS

While the distinctions between the various parrot groups are frequently blurred in local usage, nevertheless there are certain general physical characteristics which determine the group to which a parrot has been assigned.

Parrot

As we have stated, any member of the family can be correctly called a parrot. However, there are a number of species known specifically as parrots. In general, they are large stocky birds with short square tails.

Parakeet

The parakeet is the streamlined version of the parrot, small and slender, with a long graduated tail. In America the name is commonly used to denote the budgerigar, but there are many other species as well.

Servicemen away from home have an affinity for any kind of pet, and parrots are one of the most popular. This rose-breasted cockatoo flew into an army camp in New Guinea and adopted the soldiers.

Parrotlet

These are very small short-tailed South American parrots of the genus *Forpus*. They are fairly slender with square tails.

Lory

They are slimmer than the usual parrot, but otherwise quite similar, with the same square tails. Their tongues, however, are papillate (with small wart-like growths) at the tip and the mandibles (upper and lower beak) are less "toothed." They usually feed on soft fruits and the nectar of flowers.

Lorikeet

Lorikeets are to the lory what the parakeet is to the parrot—longer and slimmer, with gracefully graduated tails.

Cockatoo

The parrots in this group are probably the easiest of all to recognize because of their greater size as well as their erec-

With birds as with men, the way to the heart frequently leads through the stomach. The delicacy with which even a large parrot can take a tiny morsel of food without touching the fingers is amazing. Photo by T. Caravaglia.

"Stick training" a blue-fronted amazon. Photo by T. Caravaglia.

Most mammals cannot see colors except in shades of gray. Birds cannot only see color, they can distinguish shapes and match them accurately as this hyacinthine macaw is doing. Photo courtesy of Parrot Jungle, Florida.

The chariot race! Teach the parrot to grasp and hold on until given the cue to let go. Once he's learned this basic principle, there are any number of tricks that he can learn. Photo courtesy of Parrot Jungle, Florida.

tile crests. They are similar in shape to true parrots but are not as chunky and have deeper chests. All come from Australia or the Indo-Australian islands.

Lovebird

This type of parrot derives its name from the affection displayed between mates, but where other birds are concerned they are not always so "loving." Love birds are miniature versions of the true parrots. They are chiefly green or a delicate gray. Budgerigars are frequently, but mistakenly, called lovebirds.

Caiques

The caiques comprise a small group of species belonging to the genus *Pionites*. They are small stocky birds, often brightly colored, about nine or ten inches long, with short tails. All are native to northeastern South America.

Macaw

All of the macaws come from South and Central America. They, along with the cockatoos, are the largest members of the parrot family. They have very long pointed tails, a bare area around the eyes, a large hooked bill—so strong it can crack Brazil nuts with ease—a harsh voice and many have flamboyantly colored plumage.

Conure

These all resemble small macaws, a group to which they are closely related. However, the conures do not have the bare or unfeathered area about the eyes which is unique to the macaws. They all come from tropical America.

Cockatiel

A smaller crested bird with a long tail, it reminds one of a dwarf cockatoo. It boasts a small yellow crest. Until recently, it came in only one color—a Quaker gray—but now there is a lutino cockatiel.

Budgerigar

As everyone knows, this is the most commonly seen parakeet of them all. In America it is called simply "parakeet," although the proper name is Australian shell parakeet. In its native habitat, Australia, its color is green and yellow with black shell-like markings. In captivity it has been bred in almost every color of the rainbow except red.

"The Bird Friend," painted in the middle of the 19th century by H. Benker. While extremely ornamental cages were well known to the aristocracy, the thousands of ordinary people who loved and kept birds used cages like these seen here.

II Historical Notes

For uncounted centuries parrots large and small have been kept as pets. Perhaps they were first captured for food and for their gaudily colored feathers which were used as ornaments, but when it was discovered that the captives could "talk," their lives (and feathers) were spared. In India, if not in other lands, they were considered sacred because of this incredible ability. Early records of parrots kept as pets are to be found in Inca inscriptions and in Indian, Chinese and Persian manuscripts, as well as in the writings of the early Greeks and Romans.

The parrots' greatest appeal, of course, has always been what appears to be their uncanny ability to learn a human language. They can be taught to speak ancient Greek as easily as they can American slang. This is, as we now realize, because they mimic the sounds of human speech, and not because they understand what they are saying. I have known African and South American parrots able to "speak" three or four different languages, and what's more, keep the different tongues separated.

29

Mr. Robert Buzikowski with a variety of lories. Photo courtesy of San Diego Zoo.

A very young cockatoo that is already trained to perform in public. Photo by Dr. H. R. Axelrod.

A popular bird act, raising the flag.

Dr. Karl Russ, the noted German ornithologist, believed that the ancient Egyptians did not keep parrots since their hieroglyphics make no mention of them. He also stated that he did not believe that the Israelites kept parrots either, because he found no mention of them in the Bible. However, there is evidence that parrots were brought to Rome from Egypt during Nero's reign, and as for parrots in Israel, W.T. Greene, writing in 1893, conjectures:

> It is highly probable that the Grey Parrot was known to the Jews in the time of Solomon, whose ships, in conjunction with those of Hiram, passed, there is little doubt, between the Pillars of Hercules, and coasting southwards found the famous Ophir on that portion of the Dark Continent at present known by the general name of Guinea, whence, after an interval of three years, they returned home bringing with them among other curiosities "apes and peacocks" or parrots, as most modern commentators translate the Hebrew word *Sukeyim.*

Edward Boosey, an English authority on parrots, agrees with Greene and points out that peacocks do not come from Africa.

The first written record of parrots in history is believed to be in the writings of Ctesias, a Greek physician and historian, who lived 500 years before Christ. He described a bird called *Bittacus* that could mimic both an Indian language and Greek. From his description, modern ornithologists believe that the bird was a male plumhead or blossom-headed parakeet *(Psittacula cyanocephala).*

Aristotle, writing a century later, tells us that Alexander the Great brought parrots back to Greece after invading India, where he found them kept as pets. This species was probably *Psittacula eupatria,* now popularly known as the Alexandrine parakeet.

The Roman writer Pliny the Younger tells of parrots brought back from Syria at the time of Julius Caesar. These were presumably what are known today as the rose-ringed parakeet or ring-necked parakeet, *Psittacula krameri.* They were housed in cages of silver, ebony and tortoiseshell and were taught to speak words, especially the phrase "Ave Caesar!" (Hail Emperor!) Special slaves were assigned to train them, and when the birds graduated they were so valuable that their price exceeded the cost of their teachers. Against them Cato thundered: "O unhappy Rome! On what evil times have we fallen when we see our wives nursing puppy dogs and our men carrying parrots in their hands!"

Some time about the end of the first century A.D., Pliny wrote:

> Beyond all, Psittaci repeat men's words, and even talk connectedly. India sends this bird, which they call Psittace, with the whole body green marked only by a scarlet ring upon the nape. It will pronounce "Hail Emperor" and any words it hears; it is especially sportive after wine. The hardness of the head is the same as of the beak, and when the bird is being taught to speak, it is beaten with an iron rod, else it feels not the strokes. When it flies down it receives its weight upon its beak, and supports itself thereon; and thus lightens itself to remedy the weakness of its feet.

This curious last sentence would seem to indicate, according to Boosey, that the birds were either dazed from being hit on the head with iron rods or from the wine which they were given to drink. We are at a loss, however, to understand what benefit accrued from an inebriated bird, and unfortunately the historian does not enlighten us.

It was during this period too that the Roman poet Ovid wrote his famed elegy to his mistress Corinna's dead parrot:

> His bones a mound doth cover,
> A little mound as doth befit his size,
> And on it is a little stone
> That bears this little legend:
> From this memorial, you may see
> What love my mistress bore to me.
> Whene'er to her I spake, my words
> Meant more than any other bird's.

By the time of the emperor Heliogabalus (A.D. 218) parrots were so common in Rome that they were served as delicacies at banquets, ornamented with their own feathers, and were even fed to lions.

As the Roman empire spread over southern Europe so did the pet parrot, but the northern climes with their unheated castles were not so conducive to the tropical birds' health, and it is not until the middle of the 15th century that we first hear of one in northern Europe, and it was 1504 before the first ones were seen in England as "exotic luxuries." That they became more and more popular among the nobility and that they had "snob appeal" is evidenced by the fact that many of them were included in family portraits painted during the 17th and 18th centuries.

Long before Christopher Columbus discovered the New World, the Indians had acquired the art of taming and keeping parrots, and feathers from the brilliantly colored birds adorned their headdresses. Columbus first brought parrots back to Spain as gifts to Ferdinand and Isabella. From then on many amazons and macaws were taken back to Europe by sailors, but owing to the lack of knowledge of their requirements most of the birds did not live very long in the Old World habitat.

Today, vastly improved knowledge of bird lore and the tremendous advances of medical science have made the keeping of captive birds far less hazardous. Much is being done, both by governments and by amateurs, to preserve those species which appear to be in danger of extinction so that others will not suffer the fate of the Carolina parakeet.

Carolina Parakeets

Until the early years of this century, the United States had its own parrot, the Carolina parakeet or conure—*Conuropsis carolinensis*—the only known resident species to live in a wild state north of the Mexican border. Like the much lamented passenger pigeon, Carolina conures at one time existed in great numbers (although not so great as the pigeons) and ranged from the Great Lakes west almost to the Rocky Mountains, southward into Texas and along the Atlantic coast from Virginia to Florida.

W.T. Greene described them thus:

> The appearance of the Caroline Conure is exceedingly pleasing, the rich emerald green of the upper plumage is relieved by the vividly orange red of the forehead and cheeks, while the rest of the head and neck are gamboge (reddish yellow), and on the shoulder spots of orange red are intermixed with patches of golden yellow; the under surface of the body is yellowish green, and the outer webs of the primaries are bluish green, passing into bright yellow at the base. The legs and feet are flesh color, and the eyes light brown.

John James Audubon wrote:

> The woods are best fitted for them, and there the richness of their plumage, their beautiful mode of flight, and even their screams, afford welcome intimation that our darkest forests and most sequestered swamps are not destitute of charms.

But alas, as the woods were leveled by the encroaching pioneers and farm lands took their place, the slaughter of the birds began. The farmers organized in defense of their cultivated fields and orchards. The parakeets were doomed.

34

A Delft porcelain plaque entitled "Parrot in Cage" from 1750. It was painted brown, green, blue and red. Photo courtesy of Deutschvogelbauer Museum, Neheim-Husten.

Another factor, along with their crop depredations, which contributed to their downfall was, strange to say, their tremendous fraternal love: if one member of a flock were injured, the remainder were loath to leave their wounded comrade; consquently many more fell victim to the irate farmers' weapons than would have, had they all taken flight at the first report of a gun.

Their last small flock was seen in the Everglades (Florida) in 1904. The last known living specimen died in the Cincinnati Zoo.

"I think I'll take you home!"

III Selecting a Parrot

It is generally agreed that among the best talkers and most easily tamed parrots are the African greys. Several of the amazon species are in the same category. Next come the macaws and then the cockatoos. While almost every member of the parrot family can be taught to speak with some degree of success, it should be kept in mind that the voices of the smaller birds are weaker.

Health Indications
When buying a parrot, look for an active, healthy bird, preferably one

that likes to have its head scratched. Its eyes should be bright and its claws all there (four on each foot). Look to see that it balances well when it perches. The plumage of a first-class bird looks as if it were waxed. However, if everything else is in order, ragged feathers or even a broken tail should not scare you off. This can happen in transportation. Feathers will grow in again.

Extend the side of your hand toward the bird. If he almost falls over his own tail in his anxiety to escape, while screeching at top pitch, chances are that this bird will take longer and be more difficult to train than a bird that eyes your approach calmly. Best of all is a bird which moves slowly toward you with his beak closed.

Look for firm droppings on the bottom of the cage. Avoid any bird that suffers from diarrhea (this can be detected by noting any soiling around the vent) as it could be the symptom of a disease. A bird that sits listlessly with its feathers fluffed out or with a nodding head drooped low may also be ill.

Before making your choice it may be wise to visit several establishments and see what species are on sale. If the kind you want is not available, it can be ordered. You usually can judge the condition of a potential purchase by the condition of the pet shop. Is everything kept scrupulously clean? Are all of the other pets kept for sale in first-class condition?

The golden-winged conure or the bee bee parrot? Either of these **Brotogeris** *parakeets would be an excellent choice for a pet.*

Try to find out how old the parrot is. This is not easy, because many birds are captured as adults in the wild or have come into possession of the dealer second, third or fourth hand. A very young bird is recognizable, as is a very old one, but in between they all look alike.

There are plumage changes which take place with some but by no means all parrots between the time they leave the nest and the time they mature, and those familiar with a particular species can tell the bird's age by the extent or degree of these changes. Once the plumage has matured, the appearance of the bird will not change significantly until old age sets in. For example, the yellow area on a double yellow-head *(Amazona ochrocephala)* extends farther with each molt. Starting with a small patch on the forehead it gradually spreads until the entire head, neck and shoulders are yellow.

Telling the Age

A baby parrot leaving the nest is almost is large and as well-developed as an adult. It must be if it is to fly and seek its own living. A young bird, like a teenager, is usually slim; the bare skin around the eyes is fresh, less wrinkled and less extensive; the leg scales, a heritage from reptilian ancestors, are less noticeable. An old bird is heavier, the eye-ring and beak cere are heavy and wrinkled and the leg scales are thick and prominent. The toe, leg and wing joints become knobby.

An older, already trained bird who talks will undoubtedly cost a great deal more than an untrained young bird. However, if he does not start talking to you at once do not be disturbed, as many good talkers will not talk in the presence of strangers. There will be a period during which the parrot adapts to its new owner and home before feeling relaxed enough to talk. However, if you are paying for a talking bird, ask the dealer to warrant this fact in writing.

Young parrots are perhaps the best bet because they are, first of all, cheaper, and can be trained in the way you wish. This is not to say that a baby bird is a "must." Almost any adult, even a wild one, can with patience be tamed and taught to talk.

Small Parrots

The smaller parrots must be evaluated somewhat differently. Usually there are several in a single cage, making it difficult to select one particular bird.

Assume that the broader-breasted, bigger-headed birds are males. While this is not invariably true, it is a general rule. Again generalizing, pick the bird with the finest cere and the softest appearing leg scales.

A Mexican double yellowhead amazon parrot at the age of six weeks. This species is bred in captivity and is quite popular in the United States. Photo by L. van der Meid.

Turn the bird over and examine the vent for signs of diarrhea; this will be evidenced by stains on the vent feathers. Avoid the bird which puffs himself up like a baby chick; feathers should be down tight and hard.

Almost invariably when smaller parrots are housed together, your approach will cause them to flee to the opposite side of the cage. This is because they are social birds and if one or two are frightened, the others will imitate their behavior.

If the owner of the establishment permits, place your hand very slowly in the cage (shield the opening around your arm with the other hand so that no bird can escape) and slowly move your hand toward the level of the bird. A bird that is not too disturbed will move deliberately away from your extended hand as it approaches, while a thoroughly frightened bird will squawk and fly and batter himself against the cage.

It is quite common for the tails of the smaller parrots to shred. This is because, as they climb up and down the bars of their cage, the feathers press through, tearing the barbs. As we have stated before, these feathers will be replaced by new ones at the next molt.

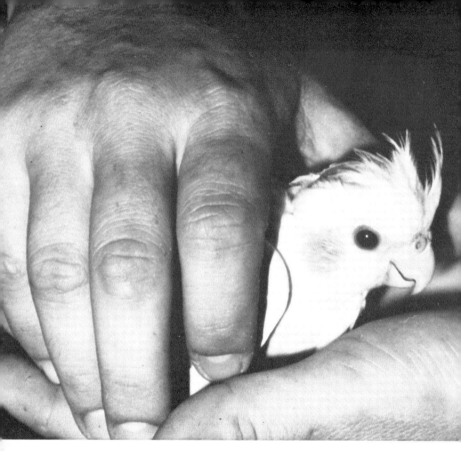

When held properly most birds will not struggle to get free. This cockatiel appears comfortable and secure in its handler's grip. Photo by Dr. H. R. Axelrod.

IV   General Care and Maintenance

Acclimating New Imports

The majority of parrots are imported from countries where the climate is sunny and warm; consequently, the birds have to adjust themselves on arrival here to differences in light and temperature.

The seasons for exporting birds fluctuate somewhat, but most birds are exported at the end of the breeding periods when young birds are plentiful. These periods usually coincide with the cold seasons in the temperate zones, when all tropical birds should be given special care and attention.

At one time all parrots came to us by sea and, although they traveled under indifferent conditions on shipboard, changes in temperature were spread out over a number of weeks. This meant that the birds were a little more adjusted to climatic changes when they were landed. Nowadays birds are shipped by air, so one day they are flying under a tropical sun and the next they are caged in a bleak country, perhaps in midwinter.

Isolation

Newly imported birds should, for their health's sake, be isolated from all other birds and, whenever possible, from each other. Sanitation is, of course, essential at all times; with newly imported specimens every cage, pen or aviary should be kept scrupulously clean even if it entails cleaning more than once daily. The person doing the cleaning should make sure that all utensils and his own hands are washed in a germicide both before and after caring for a fresh batch of birds. This will prevent the possible spread of any infection. Ammonia or one of the chlorinated disinfectants does a good job.

The room or aviary where new arrivals are housed should be kept warm and dry at an even temperature. This varies according to the species, but it should never be less than 75°F. to 80°F. (26°—28°C.) The first few weeks in their new country will have a definite bearing on the birds' ultimate happiness and life span. As soon as they arrive put them into their newly disinfected quarters and give them proper food. At this stage they should have water that has first been boiled and allowed to cool. To this add one of the good proprietary germicides or an antibiotic, using the dosage prescribed by a veterinarian. Don't guess—follow directions carefully. The sensible use of antibiotics over the past years has saved the lives of thousands of parrots.

Although parrots come from hot countries, once they get used to the climate of their new home they will be able to withstand quite low temperatures, but they can never stand drafts. Probably more sickness is brought on by drafts than by any other single cause. Although plenty of fresh air should be available to the bird, do not place the cage or stand in any direct draft, such as between outside doors or in front of windows.

Artificial Light

Newly imported birds are still accustomed to hot sunshine and long hours of daylight. Sun lamps intended for human beings can be used to supply them with additional "sunshine." It is wise, however, to have expert advice before using one of these lamps. In any event, the bird should not be exposed for more than five to ten minutes at a time (starting at five and slowly working up to ten), and it should always be free to move out of the direct glare.

If sunray lamps are not used to simulate sunshine, a beneficial effect can be achieved by artificial lighting. The hours of sunshine can be lengthened by using incandescent or fluorescent light. Self-operating time switches that turn the light on and off at set times are useful. The days can then be lengthened mornings and evenings. All birds benefit from longer periods of light which enable them to eat at more regular hours and over a longer period of time.

Do not keep any bird in the full glare of artificial light or sunlight. If housed indoors, the cage or stand should be so placed that the bird is not directly under an electric light. With regard to sunlight, although parrots like it they also like to be able to get out of its direct rays when they wish. On the other hand, it is inadvisable to house any bird where there is no sunlight at all.

Handling the New Arrival

Extreme caution must be exercised when birds are actually held in the hands. They can inflict nasty wounds. Some are, of course, more dangerous than others, but even the nectar-feeding species can bite. Since their beaks are hinged at the top, the muscles controlling the upper mandibles are very powerful. If one of these birds escapes and has to be caught, try not to frighten it, as frightened birds can inflict vicious wounds. While parrots do not have talons like birds of prey, their claws are quite sharp and strong—certainly strong enough to close painfully on a finger.

Hold the bird's head with one hand and with the other grasp him by the back, holding the wings against his sides. A panicky bird can be handled more easily if you toss a bath towel or even a coat over him first.

If the new bird arrives in a closed box, protect your hands with stout leather gloves before trying to take it out. The bird should be grasped gently but firmly, making certain that the back of the head is held first. Often it is possible to transfer a bird by opening one side of the crate and placing it against the door of the open cage. If you cover the crate with a heavy cloth, chances are the parrot will move toward the light. If not, he can be gently—I repeat, *gently*—urged out with a light stick.

After this necessary first handling, try not to handle the bird again until it has become tamer unless, of course, there is an emergency. Parrots, like elephants, have long memories and unpleasant experiences linger in their minds. I have known many birds that constantly refused to be friendly with people of one sex or the other because of an early frighten-

The proper way to hold a parrot. Photo by Dr. H. R. Axelrod.

ing experience received at the hands of a man or woman. Many parrots prefer women to men because in the native villages women and girls are charged with the responsibility of feeding and gentling the newly captured birds.

Food and Water

Newly imported parrots are usually young birds that have already been partially hand-reared by their trappers and fed on various boiled cereals, especially corn, and bananas. This applies particularly to the birds imported from South America. It is wise to continue feeding these birds the same diet they have been on for a short time, but it is essential to offer them a more normal diet as soon as possible.

Parrots as a rule do not drink much. Nevertheless, they should always have access to fresh water. I am firmly of the opinion that the newly arrived bird should be given only water that has been boiled and allowed to cool. Fouled water is one of the fastest ways of passing infection from bird to bird.

Diarrhea

New arrivals may be afflicted with diarrhea caused by the drastic change in temperature and food. Fortunately, in the majority of cases this can be remedied quickly by the use of antibiotics, correct housing, warm temperature, clean seed and fresh boiled water. If indisposed birds are slow to recover, the advice of a veterinarian should be sought immediately since the diarrhea may then indicate a more serious ailment.

Companionship

Most parrots are gregarious by nature, so single birds should not be left alone for long periods. They should be constantly visited by their owner or members of the family, particularly if no other bird is housed close by.

In my opinion, the chances of a bird becoming a truly desirable pet depend on the treatment it receives when it first arrives. Lack of companionship is almost certain to have an adverse and lasting effect.

Toys

Most parrots appreciate things to play with. This is particularly true of the smaller conures and parakeets. Toys should be limited—don't overcrowd the cage—and they should be kept scrupulously clean. Soft fabrics, rubber articles or anything dangling from strings should be avoided since a bird can quickly injure itself by getting its claws or its beak caught in the frayed fabric, hanging itself, or becoming sick from eating rubber. Toys for the larger varieties usually consist of a ball of some hard material or a short stick of wood. Some authorities recommend a well boiled bone as a plaything. The bone should be replaced daily, however, so that it will not become a breeding ground for germs. A favorite toy should never be used to tease a bird; it may turn vicious, which is the last thing any owner would want to happen.

Plumage

Although most newly imported birds are in fairly good feather, an occasional messy specimen will turn up. Such a bird can be helped by spraying it with a fine spray of clean tepid water. Spray guns suitable for birds are to be found in pet shops. All spraying should be done in the early morning so that the feathers have time to dry before the bird roosts at sundown. Damp feathers can cause loss of body heat even in a warm room, leaving the bird susceptible to chills. Aerosol bird washes are commercially available and very effective.

After several sprayings, a bird's plumage should be reasonably clean, although some of the feathers may be broken or frayed. Some owners pull these out so that new ones can develop. To my mind, this practice with newly imported birds is not desirable because the growing of new feathers imposes an unnecessary strain at a time when they need all their strength. Only when they have been fully acclimated and are being readied for exhibition do I recommend the pulling out of broken or frayed feathers.

Molting

It is natural for birds to have a complete change of plumage at least once a year, although with some tropical birds this may be extended over quite a period of time that varies with individual birds and, of course, with different species. During the molting period be particularly careful to protect the birds from drafts and dampness, because at this time their resistance is definitely lowered.

When birds are molting I always remove the cast feathers. I feel that if they have the opportunity of playing with their molted feathers it can lead to their developing into "feather pluckers" constantly picking at their own or other birds' feathers. Sometimes a bird sheds an incredible number of feathers, judging by the quantity in and about his cage. This is perfectly normal. However, at no time should he show bare areas or completely lose his ability to fly. These are abnormal conditions requiring investigation to determine their cause. It is during a molt that cut, broken or damaged feathers are cast off. A cut or broken feather does not heal itself; a new one just grows in when the old one drops.

Liberty

I am often asked if it is advisable to give a pet bird liberty indoors or out. This depends to a great extent on the bird itself and the surroundings, but I do think that if it is at all possible the bird will benefit if it is allowed occasional unrestricted freedom. As a general rule tame parrots do not fly very much. They much prefer to clamber about from place to place. They should, of course, be watched if they are let loose in a room full of furniture. A bird will learn quickly that it can come out of its cage and play on the floor with its owner. But it is unwise to let a bird loose entirely on its own; the temptation to gnaw on everything it encounters will become too strong, resulting in all kinds of mischief. A bird can be allowed freedom out of doors if the yard or garden is surrounded by a good high wall or fence and the bird is kept under careful observation. This sort of liberty should be planned to avoid unforeseen contingencies. I have known many African greys, amazons and macaws to spend a great deal of time out of doors. In some cases the birds were placed on a large tree stump where they could have their food and water and generally enjoy themselves in the fresh air. A great deal of fun can be enjoyed by letting a really tame bird loose in the garden, even if it is only for short periods of time. Late afternoon or early evening is the best time for taking your bird outdoors. There is less inclination to "take off" into the dusk.

Squawking

Parrots are noted for their raucous voices. The cries of birds living in

A blue and gold macaw (left) and a scarlet macaw (right) squawking at each other in an aviary of a bird farm. Photo by L. van der Meid.

a society like theirs are used to signal the other birds. This is important when danger threatens the flock. It serves two purposes: it alerts other members of the flock to danger, and the mass screeching hopefully frightens off the approaching predator or at least discourages him by letting him know that he's been sighted.

The thing to remember is that you should never *encourage* your parrot's squawking. The surest way of turning him into a chronic squawker is to tease and frighten him. Normally, a parrot does not squawk until teased, frightened or annoyed. There is another situation which sometimes arises with a parrot kept inside the house. This occurs when a bird squawks for one reason or another and the owner runs immediately to see what's wrong. Any parrot, particularly a tame one, will enjoy this extra attention and will quickly learn that squawking brings his owner to his side. The answer is *not* to make a fuss over the bird when he squawks; if possible, ignore him. If the parrot persists, take a blanket and cover the cage. The darkness will act as a punishment and discourage further raucous cries.

Escaped Birds

Never chase a bird that is fluttering about a room. If it is dashing itself against a window pane and you have no net at hand, get a soft old Turkish towel (not a coarse one) and toss or drop it over the bird. Then gently pick up the bird in its folds. But take it easy and make no sudden movements. If you don't catch the bird the first time, wait until it quiets down before you make another attempt.

If the bird escapes at night, turn off the lights in the room and use a flashlight. Parrots do not like to fly in the dark.

If the bird flies out of doors, put food close to the house, on a window sill or, if it is housed outdoors, on top of the aviary. Keep everything as quiet as possible and wait for the bird to come down and feed. Douse it with water from the garden hose to keep it from flying away. You can be ready with a piece of netting or a Turkish towel to toss over it.

If you locate the stray at a distance, go after it with a feeding trap (the old schoolboy trick of a baited box supported by a peg to which a lengthy cord is attached may work). If the errant bird has a mate, use it as a decoy. Failing all else, follow the bird quietly until it settles for the night, hopefully in an accessible location. Parrots are reluctant to fly in the dark, and if you move quietly the escapee can be approached.

A net comes in handy for catching most small birds, including smaller parrots, but it must always be used with care. Photo by L. van der Meid.

This elaborate cage was made of flat wire and wood, about 1670. In recent years it has been used as a film prop. The cage is about 40 inches high and the circular turret is about 55 inches in diameter. Photo courtesy of Deutschvogelbauer Museum, Neheim-Husten.

V Cages and Aviaries

As we have repeatedly pointed out, the parrot family is so extensive that it includes birds of every size from the tiny hanging parrots of the Philippines to the tremendous and majestic macaws and cockatoos. It should be obvious, then, that housing arrangements for the individual species will differ widely in size, design and construction.

The salient design of all housing—cage or aviary—must consider the health, comfort and happiness of the birds. Esthetic pleasure and convenience to the owners, while important, should be secondary considerations. Well-housed birds will become tamer, their feathers will stay in better condition and they will live longer. Some species can have their beautiful appearance spoiled if they are not able to spread their tremendous wings.

Cages

No parrot cage can be too large; many of them are too small. Even the smaller birds—shell parakeets or budgies, for instance—are happier in a large cage. The larger members of the family, such as cockatoos and macaws, for convenience are sometimes kept on stands.

It is difficult to build a parrot cage (a cage, not an aviary) at home, as they should be sturdily constructed of metal. A parrot can gnaw its way out of a wooden cage or a wicker one in no time. The metal should not be enameled as the paint will disappear quickly and the metal beneath will rust. Undoubtedly the cages manufactured today are extremely serviceable. These cages, either round or square in shape, are constructed of good quality steel wire galvanized or plated and welded into a solid, almost indestructible, unit.

Wire cages come in many different sizes and, of course, custom-made ones can be ordered to accommodate any particular bird or pair of birds. The sizes suitable for the larger Amazon parrots and the big cockatoos should not be less than, say, some 20 to 22 inches at the base and up to 36 inches high. For the African greys, smaller Amazons, large conures, etc., a base of 18 to 20 inches square and a height of up to 30 inches is desired. The smaller conures, ringnecks and so forth need a base of some 15 to 18 inches square and up to 28 inches high. The parrotlets, small parakeets, lovebirds and the like thrive very well in the large all-metal cages generally sold for the ever-popular budgerigars.

The latter type of cage has a movable metal tray; the others have stout wire grillwork at the bottom above the movable tray section. The reasons for this are twofold: first, to keep the birds from the actual cage bottom, and second, to prevent an escape while the tray is being cleaned.

There are some experienced parrot keepers, however, who disagree about the wire grill on the cage bottom. They believe that the birds should be able to rest their feet on a flat surface. Sometimes a compromise is reached by placing a clump of grassy turf on the grill on which the birds can rest their feet.

Since they feed on nectar and fruit, lories and lorikeets need a specially designed cage to prevent the fouling of the surrounding areas by their food and droppings. These species are usually housed in box-type cages with sand-filled drawers. A wire grill may be fitted above the drawers. Sand drawers need to be covered with absorbent paper sheets that can be changed daily or oftener if necessary.

Paper or other disposable material like coarse sawdust, cat litter or crumbled peat moss may be used in the trays with wire grills. The advantage of the grill is that it helps to keep the birds from fouling themselves while climbing about in their cages.

Whatever type of cage is used, it is important that the door has a locking mechanism which cannot be opened by the bird. Parrots are clever, and with their strong beaks they can easily undo any ordinary door fastener. An escape can be disastrous. Pet shops sell a special type of cage fastener that cannot be opened by birds.

Perches

Perches are generally made of hardwood with metal-bound ends. I often wonder if these are right for parrots, although I know they please their owners. What I am about to say applies to all kinds of perches. Parrots like to exercise their beaks, but if their perches are practically indestructible they cannot. Consequently, as soon as the birds are out of their cages they find some convenient woodwork to gnaw on, much to the annoyance of their owners. Because of this gnawing tendency, they are frequently kept permanently confined in their cages, which is unfortunate.

I think birds should be given perches that they can gnaw on. Such damaged perches will have to be renewed periodically, causing some minor inconvenience perhaps, but the birds will benefit considerably. Not that they should be given softwood perches to destroy immediately; there are many reasonably hard woods like apple, pear, plum, cherry, hawthorn, citrus fruit and nut trees, to mention only a few that are easily obtainable. Branches from these trees should be well-seasoned and dried before using them for parrot perches. It is desirable to have perches of varying thicknesses to prevent stiffness of the feet caused by always grasping perches of one size.

If regular perches are used, give the bird something additional to gnaw on such as the hardwood branches mentioned above or, if they are not available, a wooden thread spool.

Food Cups

Water and seed containers should be placed high enough so that droppings do not soil their contents, and they should be refillable from the outside. Needless to say, they should be cleaned thoroughly each day.

Since parrots are inclined to be messy with their food and droppings, plastic or glass cage-guards will help to keep the area surrounding the cage more presentable. A piece of cuttlebone should be attached to the cage. It helps to keep the birds' beaks worn down, and the minerals in it are needed for nutrition.

Stands

Because of their size, some macaws and cockatoos are kept on T-shaped stands fitted with a large sand tray below. The birds are attached by light steel chains which allow them full movement on the perches. Once they are trained to remain on the stand, the chains can be dispensed with. The stands are usually constructed of metal, either galvanized, painted or plated, with a hardwood perch and metal-lined food and water cups fixed at each end. Large birds seem to prefer stands to cages since it gives them plenty of opportunity to climb about and flap their wings. Birds on stands can be moved from place to place, or, when the weather is warm enough, they can be taken outside to add color to the yard or garden.

Birds must be trained to the chain by degrees. Unless they are, the first reaction of a bird who finds himself on an open perch is to "take off," only to be brought up short on reaching the end of the chain. Parrots have remarkably strong legs, but if the chain is long enough for the bird to pick up momentum, he can hurt himself. Until the parrot is aware of his limitations, it is best to keep the chain short.

Keep the bird caged and fix the ring to the leg. Later attach a short piece of fine chain which in due course is lengthened and finally fastened to the perch. The bird should then be allowed to move from the cage to the stand of his own free will. I have seen many hundreds of parrots tethered in this manner, and they all appeared happy and contented. When weather permits, parrots can be tethered in the open to old tree trunks or garden walls. This really gives them a change that they will enjoy.

Baths

Not all parrots like to bathe, which can present a problem since bathing is good for their plumage. It is possible to obtain large metal baths which are designed to hang over the open doors of cages. However, some birds will not use them, preferring to bathe outside their cage in a flat shallow pan. Since parrots like to splash, owners must take precautions that nothing which can be damaged by water is nearby. Some parrots have their own special ideas on bathing; some birds actually learn to clamber up to the sink and turn on the water themselves! This can of course be disastrous if hot water comes out.

After the birds have bathed, see that they are thoroughly dry before nightfall and that they are not subjected to drafts. Some owners spray their birds with water. I have known many parrots which appreciated a fine spray. In warm weather bird and cage can be put out in the rain. Be sure to remove the seed and water cups and sand tray so that the cage can be dried easily when it is brought indoors.

Location

The location of the cage is important. Parrots do not like to be left alone—they want to be with the family and like to feel that they are a part of the activity. The cage should be in a sunny spot but not in direct sun unless it is at least partially shaded. A patch of sun and a patch of shade are ideal, but allow for the movement of the sun. Even though parrots are from the tropics, in nature they limit the length of time they spend in direct sun. Choose an area that is free of drafts. Avoid placing the cage in a line between two windows or two open doors or in a passageway onto which an outside door opens.

Unless the temperature of the room drops considerably during the night, the cage need not be covered.

Aviaries

If you are going into parrot keeping on a larger scale or if you intend to try breeding parrots, you will of course want to have an aviary. This can range from a huge brick and steel glass-domed building in its own landscaped plot to the screened-off area of an attic. Existing outbuildings like garages, barns or chicken houses can be adapted to the purpose, or you can start from scratch and erect an entirely new building. Much depends upon your own ingenuity.

Basically, an aviary consists of an enclosed sleeping chamber protected from the elements, to which is attached an outdoor "flight." This flight in its simplest form can consist of a wood frame covered at the sides and roof with strong wire mesh. The mesh should cover all exposed wood. In inclement weather the birds can retire to the enclosed sleeping chamber, while in pleasant weather the flight will permit them to enjoy the sun and fresh air at will.

Locating the Aviary

Carefully consider where to place the aviary before you begin to build it. It should be located in an area that is dry and out of the prevailing wind. It should not be under trees whose foliage will drip onto it. If you can have it facing the morning sun, so much the better. However, direct sun is bad, particularly in the summer. The aviary can be shaded by a planting of vines around it, but these should be planted to grow up net-

This lovely aviary setting was photographed in California where people enjoy bringing the outdoors indoors. Photo by L. van der Meid.

ting placed about a foot from the aviary, not on the aviary wire itself since the birds will chew up the leaves.

Permanent or Temporary

Some experienced parrot keepers recommend a movable aviary in preference to one that is permanently fixed, especially if it has an earthen floor. Soil becomes foul and disease-infected over a period of time and then almost impossible to clean, no matter how much attention is paid to sanitation. Sometimes, and particularly so after a bout of infection, moving the entire aviary to another site is the only satisfactory solution. If the building is to be permanently located, then easily flushed and scoured cement flooring is the only hygienic answer to the problem.

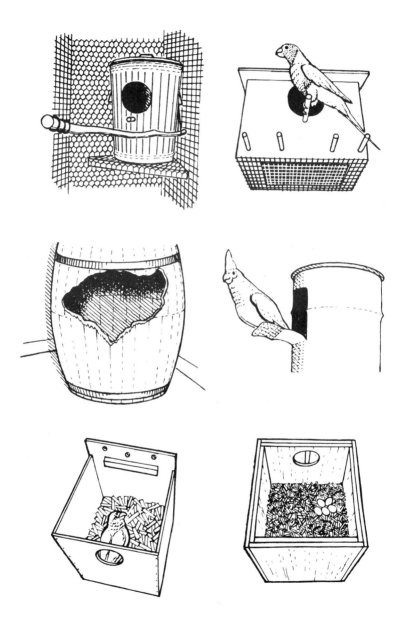

Nest boxes for various types of parrots. The tops of the lower two have been removed so that the interior can be seen. Illustrations by M. Youens.

Size

The bigger the aviary, the better. One for larger parakeets should be about 20 feet long, 6 feet wide, and 6 feet high. For parrots, macaws and cockatoos the length should be extended to at least 25 feet and the height to 8 feet. Approximately one-fourth of this space can be devoted to the shelter, the other three-fourths to the flight. In colder climates, if the birds are to be wintered outdoors the shelter will of course have to be insulated and weather-proofed. It should be whitewashed regularly on the inside, although the exterior can be decorated in any way you wish—provided there is nothing harmful which the birds can reach and gnaw.

Parrots with less powerful beaks such as parakeets, lovebirds, lories and the like can be safely housed in parakeet-type aviaries if they are made of good quality boards and stout gauge wire mesh netting. It is always advisable to double-wire portions of the outside flights and to cover with wire netting all wooden timbers and siding that come within reach of the birds' beaks. These precautions taken during construction will prevent any disappointing escapes.

When housing the larger parrots, parakeets, macaws and cockatoos, special precautions have to be taken to prevent the birds from escaping. These strong-beaked species can slice through ordinary wire mesh netting with the greatest of ease, and they will certainly do so if given the opportunity! The normal soft woods used in chicken coop construction will quickly be reduced to splinters. It is now possible to get inch-square heavy gauge metal-link fencing and welded metal rods for covering outside flights of parrot aviaries. If the shelter or sleeping section is built of brick or cement slabs, it will be practically indestructible—even by the most powerful of parrots. If built of wood, it is essential to use very thick seasoned hardwood shielded on the inside (I repeat, *inside*) with sheet metal or heavy gauge wire netting.

Flooring

Flooring should be considered carefully. Letting the earth serve as the floor is usually considered first, but it has many disadvantages; extra precautions against disease and vermin will have to be taken if this is done. For hygienic reasons, I recommend that the floor of both flight and sleeping quarters be cemented over or covered with concrete slabs. Slabs are particularly practical since they can be easily moved if the aviary is taken down and moved. These floors can be covered with a thick layer of fine washed gravel which can be raked over periodically to keep them tidy looking. Small areas clear of the perch can be seeded

Many manufacturers design the cage doors so that when opened they form a platform, permitting the bird to go in and out at will. This half-moon parrot can't seem to make up his mind whether to go in or stay out. Photo by L. van der Meid.

with grass. Many species spend much time in these grassy plots and get great enjoyment from them. If it is not possible to grow these grassy areas naturally, provide them in movable boxes; this works well with parakeets when they are kept mainly for breeding purposes.

With aviaries that have earthen floors in the flight portions there must be protection against vermin. This can be achieved by setting L-shaped strips of bituminous tar-coated small-mesh wire netting to a depth of twelve inches down into the ground all around the flights. This will have the added advantage of preventing any adventurously inclined birds from digging themselves out of the flights. It is not usual to think of birds digging, but some do, and this means of escape must be guarded against.

Doors

Whether the entrance into the aviary is through the shelter or through the flight, or both, it should be provided with a "safety" door. This is simply two doors with space enough between to close one door while the other is opened, in order to prevent the escape of the birds. There should also be a narrow door between the shelter and the flight which can be left open, except in cold weather, for the birds to come and go at will.

Planting

While it is highly desirable from an esthetic point of view to landscape the flight of an aviary, this is almost impossible to do since almost all of the members of the parrot family like to chew. You can, of course, keep planting and replanting (as long as none of the plants are poisonous), but most parrot keepers soon give this up as a lost cause. Perhaps the best compromise is a small plot kept planted with mixed grass and grain seeds at one end of the flight, but not under a perch or perching branch. Dead trees can be erected and hollow logs and stumps strategically placed to add a picturesque effect and to serve as nests for some species.

Aviary Perches

The main perches should be made of seasoned hardwood branches. They will then not need to be renewed very often. However, a few soft or greenwood branches with the bark left on should also be provided to give the birds something to gnaw on to amuse themselves. If bits of wood are swallowed (provided it is non-poisonous) they will be beneficial. A shortage of material to chew on may account for some birds being intolerant toward their owners and for pulling out their own feathers. If metal tubing or baked enamel piping is fixed at convenient angles to the floor, these extra perches can be attached so that they are firm and solid but easily removed and replaced.

This trainer, returning a group of birds from exhibition, will carefully place each one on its personal perch. Photo by L. van der Meid.

It is wise to locate perches at the ends of the flight in order to give the birds a free open flyway with the fewest encumbrances. If the flight can be built around a dead tree stump or if such a rotting stump can be "planted" in a convenient location inside the flight, your birds will be even happier.

Perches should always be placed far enough away from the sides of the aviary to prevent the birds' tails from brushing against the wire netting. Sometimes swings and hoops are installed in the flights, but I believe that good straightforward natural perches are appreciated more.

Aviary Baths

It is relatively simple to arrange shallow bathing areas in flighted aviaries. Such baths can be ornamental, adding to the general beauty. The bathing pools should be shallow and easy to clean. For this reason they should never be placed below perches or they will become fouled. Shallow vessels should have their bottoms roughened so that the bathing birds can get a firm grip; they object to slipping and sliding. The water should be replaced at least once a day. A garden hose can be used to flush out the baths and refill them. Flowing water, if it can be arranged, is not only attractive but also sanitary.

Feeders and Waterers

Use containers that are indestructible but easily washed and sterilized. Avoid any made of metals that might rust and any made of wood that would be quickly reduced to chips. Ceramic or glass cups or bowls are probably the wisest choice. Pet shops will offer you a wide selection. Many owners prefer to use the gravity type of waterer for the smaller birds because the water cannot be fouled. This is merely a stoppered bottle from which a metal tube protrudes. It is hung upside down and the bird "licks" water from the end of the tube.

The placement of food and water containers should be carefully considered. They should not be in spots where they can be fouled by the caged birds' droppings or by the droppings of wild birds flying overhead or resting on top of the aviary. They must also be protected from inclement weather and wind, as a gust of wind can easily scatter the light seed. A corner is bad since it will permit one or two birds to get to the food dish first, devour all the choicest tidbits and keep the less belligerent birds away. This leaves us with the center of the flight, which is, all in all, the wisest alternative. The container should be raised from the floor (particularly so if it is an earthen floor which can get muddy) and placed in the center of a shallow box in which the discarded husks can accumulate. Holders for cuttlebone, mineral blocks and gravel will also have to be arranged.

Parrots are like children in that they enjoy those extra little attentions.

VI Feeding

When it comes to feeding, the vast array of parrots can be roughly divided into two general categories—those whose staple diet consists of seeds and those whose chief foods are nectar and soft fruits. Correct feeding cannot be too strongly emphasized since it is so tremendously important in keeping the birds happy and healthy. There are, of course, many brands of good packaged foods available in pet shops, and their use is advised for those species for which they were formulated.

When new birds are bought I always ask the vendor what they have been fed and continue with that food until I can accustom them to my own diet. Sudden drastic changes in diet can quickly upset any bird's digestion, with far-reaching results.

Seed-eaters

Owners of seed-eating birds should always endeavor to provide their pets with good balanced diets, constantly bearing in mind that what is suitable for the bird in its wild state is not necessarily right under captive conditions. When flying free in the wild, birds vary their food at will and, of course, burn up calories at a tremendous rate with the amount of exercise they get. In captivity birds are housed in restricted quarters and seldom have the opportunity to get anywhere near their needed quota of natural exercise. This being so, their food should be controlled so that they do not eat large quantities of highly fattening foods. Problems can easily be caused by too much rich food. I am afraid that the health of too many pets has been adversely affected by the overindulgence of their loving owners. Overrich feeding does, I feel, contribute in many cases to feather problems. If birds are kept in large aviaries with plenty of flying space they will, of course, need more of these richer foods to restore the energy they expend.

Along with many other experienced parrot keepers, I must warn against indulging the birds exclusively with sunflower seeds. A diet consisting of only these is far too fattening. It will result in obesity, poor plumage and overgrown beak and claws, and there will be other signs of poor nutrition. Sunflower seeds, and peanuts as well, are much loved by the seed-eating birds—they will eat them to the exclusion of everything else that their system requires if their owners permit it—but such seeds should be only a portion of their diet or saved for treats and not fed routinely.

Larger Parrots

For the larger birds such as the various amazons, African greys, cockatoos and macaws, I have found the following seed mixture most suitable. It is enjoyed by the great majority of these birds. Use one-third best quality large canary seed, one-third mixed sunflower and safflower seed, with the remaining third made up of equal parts of peanuts (shelled or unshelled), maize or sweet corn, dari or milo and buckwheat. Sometimes as a change a few plump hulled oats or groats can be substituted for one of the cereals mentioned. This mixture gives the birds quite a variety of seeds that together make up a balanced diet.

The following mixture is recommended as being highly suitable for parrots:

Rolled oats	20%
Whole-wheat meal	20%
Soybean oil meal	20%
Peanut oil meal	10%
Yellow corn meal	10%
Buttermilk (dry)	5%
Brewer's yeast (dry)	5%
Alfalfa leaf meal	5%
Oyster shell flour	2%
Iodized salt	2%
Cod liver oil concentrated	1%

To nine parts of this mixture add one part cooked ground horse meat and gravy. Allow it to cool and solidify in pans, refrigerate and use as required. Horse meat, of course, can be purchased canned or frozen in pet food departments.

Added Protein

Recent research into parrot nutrition seems to indicate that the birds need more protein in their diet than was formerly supposed. Many breeders believe that ailments like French molt and tumors are caused by a lack of protein. It can certainly do no harm to enrich any parrot's diet with a limited amount of ground or chopped meat, either fresh or out of a can of all-meat dog food.

Poultry raisers are all familiar with the commercially prepared food known as chick-starter ration. This is a high-protein food designed for young growing chickens. It is very good for parrots, too, especially the nestlings, if they can be tempted to eat it. This can often be accomplished by mixing the ration with sieved cooked egg and freshly grated carrot.

Fruits and Vegetables

To keep the birds in perfect health, seed mixtures have to be supplemented with fresh fruits, nuts and many green leafy vegetables. Partiality to different vegetables and fruits varies. Like humans, parrots have their likes and dislikes. All fresh foods should be carefully washed to eliminate any residual insecticides.

Some birds prefer sweet apples; others choose ripe pears. Again, oranges and grapefruit are accepted readily by many birds, as are bananas, figs, plums, dates and other soft fruits. Grapes, both black and white, are great favorites, and many owners get much amusement from watching their birds peeling grapes, extracting the pips and generally having a fine time with the pulp.

The amount of fruit given must, of course, be carefully controlled or there will be digestive upsets. The fruit should be as varied as possible so that the birds do not become too fond of one particular kind and refuse to eat any other. After fruit has been eaten, any refuse should be carefully cleaned up so that the bird does not get its feathers messy and the uneaten fruit become sour.

When fresh fruit is not readily available, dried fruits can be substituted; most birds will eat them. Usually they must be soaked before being offered.

All parrots, even the big ones, seem to enjoy the various seedling grasses. Without a doubt these grasses contain large quantities of valuable vitamins, and every endeavor should be made to encourage the birds to eat them. Pots of growing greens that can be attached to cages are available. Such things as chickweed *(Cerastium)*, plantain heads *(Plantago)*, dock seeds *(Rumex)*, sow thistles *(Sonchus)*, young dandelion leaves *(Taraxadum)*, endive, the various cabbages and spinach can be offered in rotation. Of the root vegetables, carrots are probably the most valuable and generally liked.

Care must be taken to keep birds away from flowers or house plants since many of these have an undesirable effect when eaten. This is particularly true of geraniums, philodendrons and cacti and succulents. The cacti may be quite harmless in themselves but they often have sharp and undetectable spines that can damage the tongue. The macaws are very partial to nuts, especially Brazil nuts, which the birds crack and open with their powerful beaks. Some birds like one variety, some another, but it does not take the owner very long to find out which. Not only are they a nutritious food because of their oil content, but the birds derive much pleasure from cracking their shells. I have many times seen parrots play with nuts before eating them, much as a cat plays with a mouse.

Harmful Foods

I must warn owners against giving their birds human foods like candy, sugar, bacon rind, cakes, cookies and so forth. Although they may eat them and appear to like them, such foods are not good for birds. I have known many birds to develop bad digestive conditions through being allowed to eat such foods. In addition, they may well be the cause of feather plucking. If the birds are to be treated while you dine, they should be given their favorite fruit or nut tidbit. I realize that birds love to eat with their owners and togetherness helps to keep them happy and contented.

Medium Parrots

The smaller parrots, the large conures and the large parakeets will, of course, need a slightly different mixture of seeds. The following blend will be readily accepted by all species if slight adjustments are made to fit in with individual needs. Use 50% best quality large canary seed, 25% safflower and mixed sunflower seed and 25% large white millet, hemp, dari or milo, buckwheat, hulled oats (or groats) in equal proportions. This particular mixture is suitable all the year 'round as it contains a balanced vitamin and calorie content. Seed mixtures which can serve as a basic diet are also commercially available.

Most of the fresh fruits and various green foods mentioned before are suitable for the smaller birds. In addition, they can be offered dates, fresh figs, ripe sweet cherries, raspberries, loganberries, blackberries, fresh green oats and seeding chickweed. Not all of these will be appreciated by every bird, but with trial and error the owner can narrow down its preferences. Dried raisins, currants and various nuts can be offered as a change from fresh fruits. Here again some will be refused while others will be taken readily. Many species are extremely fond of millet in the natural sprays and these will often be eaten by birds which are feeling a little out of condition even when they refuse other foods. It is important, I think, to always keep a supply of good plump millet sprays on hand.

The drinking cups must be cleaned each day and refilled with fresh water. Bathing water should be kept entirely separate. As with the larger birds, mixed gravel of a suitable size should always be within reach of the birds. This together with cuttlebone and mineral blocks will supply the needed traces of mineral.

Small Parrots

The dwarf parrots, small conures, small parakeets, lovebirds, etc., will thrive on a seed mixture made up of 50% mixed canary seed, 25% mixed millet seed (excluding red millet) and 25% of a mixture of equal parts of hemp, sunflower, safflower and hulled oats or groats. For a change, rolled oats can be substituted for the hulled oats or groats. It is wise to increase the amount of canary seed for young birds and increase the proportion of millet for adults. Those persons with only a few birds should purchase seed in small quantities so that it is always fresh.

The various fresh fruits and green foods listed for the larger species can be offered to all the smaller birds. Once again I emphasize the need

This black-capped lory is one of the nectar-feeding species. To help keep the cage clean, his owner hand-feeds him, a process which both enjoy. Photo by H. Müller.

to remove all fruits and green foods that are uneaten at the end of the day. If this is not done the cages will become smelly, and the birds will be eating fouled food. Mixed gravel, cuttlebone and mineral blocks are, of course, needed for these birds, too.

The Nectar-feeding Species

There are in the parrot family a number of more delicate species whose chief diet does not consist of seeds. These are the lories and lorikeets, pigmy parrots, hanging parrots, fig parrots and a few species of the strange New Zealand parrots.

Their tongues are adapted to feeding on the pollen and nectar of flowers and on the flowers themselves, although their beaks are hooked in much the same way as those of the seed-eaters. These species can exist for a short time on an exclusive diet of seeds, and since seed mixtures are easier to use, a few uninformed importers feed them—to the detriment of the bird's health. Paralysis of the legs or fits can result.

The staple diet should be a kind of "milk sop." Mix two teaspoonfuls of condensed milk, one tablespoonful of fresh clear honey and half a teaspoonful of Mellins, with four or five tablespoonfuls of hot boiling water. The amount of water can vary according to the consistency of the liquid to be prepared, but in every case it should be boiling. The mixture should then be allowed to cool. It can be thickened by adding a small quantity of finely ground cracker meal or softened bread crumbs. In some localities where hummingbirds are frequent visitors, pet shops sell a hummingbird mixture. This is also good for the nectar-feeding parrots.

Nectar, however, is not these birds' sole diet. They also need soft fruits and some insect food to keep them in good condition.

Soak fresh fruit several hours or overnight to soften it. Grapes, bananas, raisins, cherries and berries are all good, as are dried dates and figs if well soaked. To save time, canned fruit salad or the fruits prepared for babies and sold in small jars may be served. So can stewed fruits and applesauce. Fruit or sponge cake soaked in condensed milk or in honey diluted with water is also good.

Fresh greens should be offered whenever possible. Dandelions, spinach, lettuce, celery and beet tops are good. In summer, you can give them freshly picked flowers from the garden. In winter, give a few drops of cod liver oil; one aviary I know of hangs up rashers of bacon.

Since all of these food are highly perishable, they should be prepared fresh each day; in hot weather it may be necessary to prepare them twice a day. Extreme care should be taken to clean up after the birds and to keep their cages or aviaries immaculate. Food cups should be scalded thoroughly before reusing them. It is impossible to be too zealous about all this.

In their wild state some species eat grubs and insects. This want can be filled in captivity by using mealworms, which many pet shops carry for fish food, or a good brand of bird food prepared for mynahs and other soft-billed birds. Use as directed on the package.

Gravel and Cuttlebone

In addition to all these foods, birds must have gravel and added minerals. Too many birds suffer from the lack of these essentials. Gravel is swallowed by birds; it takes the place of teeth in masticating their food. The gravel passes into the gizzard, where it grinds the seeds. The gravel itself gradually loses its effectiveness and has to be regularly replaced, therefore all seed-eating birds should have a constant supply. Gravel can be obtained in various grades and in different mixtures.

This cage is equipped with a clip-on holder for the cuttlebone. Photo by V. Serbin.

Such things as crushed flint, oyster shells, limestone and natural washed gravel grit can all be obtained in pet shop mixtures.

In addition to gravel, the birds like bits of cuttlebone and mineral blocks. These help to keep their beaks worn down to a reasonable length. The minerals they contain are absorbed into the system and provide the birds with the trace elements they need, particularly when molting and growing new feathers. Since it takes a long time for the birds to build up the necessary reserve of these salts and minerals, it is essential that a supply be kept before them constantly, not just prior to molting.

Cod Liver Oil

Unless a ready-prepared mineral-vitamin food supplement for birds is used, cod liver oil should be supplied daily. It can be added to the seeds by mixing them in it in the proportion of one teaspoonful of oil to a pound of mixed seeds. The seeds should then be kept in a jar with a tight lid and stored in the refrigerator. Cod liver oil quickly oxidizes and becomes rancid, so always be sure of its freshness and do not allow the treated seeds to remain in the seed cup overnight.

Oil can also be supplied by dropping a few drops on a piece of bread. Cod liver oil, however, can never completely take the place of sunlight as a supplier of vitamin D, and birds should be exposed to the sun as often as possible—not hot sun, of course, or sun shining through a glass window, as glass filters out the active rays which stimulate the production of vitamin D by the ergosterol in the birds' skin.

Routine

Each bird should be given just a little more than it will eat each day to allow for wastage. The seed cups should be emptied daily and the birds given a fresh supply; this will prevent the seeds from growing stale and the cup from becoming full of hulls. Poor quality or stale seed can quickly upset even a healthy bird. After a short time the owner will know the exact quantity to feed, and then only a very little will be wasted.

Almost any kind of seed can be sprouted in the home. Sprouts can be eaten from the earlier stages (upper photo) to later when the leaves are already formed (lower photo). Photos by Dr. H. R. Axelrod.

A parrot does not eat the entire seed; he cracks the shell and extracts the meat with the powerful but sensitive tongue. The husks are dropped. This may deceive you into thinking the seed dish is full, and it may very well be full—of useless hulls. So don't take any chances. Empty the dish each day and refill it with fresh clean seeds.

Water

Parrots should have fresh water constantly available. Don't just add more to the container; wash and refill it daily. For many years there was a mistaken belief that some parrots did not drink water. It is true that some do drink very little, as they get most of their requirements from the fresh fruits and green vegetables that they eat. It is also true that some species reuse the water already in their system instead of excreting it. This is why their droppings are normally semi-solid.

It is possible, however, that a newly imported parrot may not have been given water by its native captors, and sudden unlimited quantities may prove harmful. If you know that your new pet is a recent arrival from the tropics, it might be wise to limit its water at the beginning by removing the cup each day as soon as you have seen it drink. But do this only for the first few days.

The water cups should be kept scrupulously clean and not allowed to become fouled. Unclean water is one of the fastest ways of spreading infection from bird to bird. Run your finger or a brush around the inside of the cup each time you change the water. Too many people just pour out the old water and refill the cup without bothering to clean it.

Feeding Habits

Birds assimilate their food rapidly. Their digestive tract is short and the food passes through in a few hours, but 90% of the food intake is digested and absorbed. This is why birds seem to be—and are—eating almost all the time. They eat little but they eat often. There should *always* be seed in their food cup.

The smaller birds, shell parakeets especially, will starve to death if they are deprived of food for only two days. This is why it is important to feed all birds every day, and why it is particularly important to be sure that what appear to be seeds in the feeding dish are not merely the hulls of seeds already eaten. Nor should familiar food be completely replaced by a new variety until it is known positively that the bird is eating it.

Contrary to some so-called "expert" opinion, a sick bird should never be fasted. Quite the contrary, it should be tempted to eat as much as it will.

At a parrot circus in California. The trainer's stick is used to pick up the bird and to give cues. The macaw placing the rings on the upright watches the trainer for approval. Photo by L. van der Meid.

VII So You Want to Train a Parrot!

Parrots, someone once remarked, "are the most dog-like of birds." This is not because they bark, although they can be taught to do so, but because of their measured and considered actions. It is interesting to observe the way pet parrots will study a situation before acting because they seem to understand what is going on about them and then gauge their actions accordingly.

Other types of birds seem nervous and flighty; approach them too closely and they dart away. Even when confined to a cage, most birds will flutter against the bars in panic if you put your hand up to them. The only things they seem to be interested in are the daily processes of living—eating, sleeping and, if given the opportunity, reproducing.

Not so friend parrot. When you approach a caged parrot, even an untamed bird, he will cock his head and study you. Approach him too closely and, if newly caught he'll warn you by opening his mouth threateningly and emitting his harsh raucous cry. Continue your approach and he'll back off, spreading his wings to make himself look larger, at the same time speeding up the tempo and volume of his warning. If you should persist and he is cornered, he will throw himself on his back, which is a defensive posture. In this position he can, with his powerful claws, seize, hold and then bite. He will also screech at the top of his lungs to warn the members of his flock of danger.

We are referring now, of course, to the larger parrots, macaws and cockatoos. You will notice also that all through this performance he keeps his eye on *you*, and that busy brain of his is at all times calculating whether to bluff, fight or flee. The response of a tamed bird is, of course, considerably different. As you approach, if he knows you he will move closer and incline his head in a dignified manner to be scratched. This denotes trust, because when he bows his head he cannot watch you. Extend your hand and he will gravely lift his claw, not to shake hands—but to slowly climb aboard. Again you will notice that he constantly searches your face and observes all your actions for a clue to your motives.

This ability to observe and organize his thoughts in accordance with the situation is what differentiates the parrot's intelligence from that of most birds. In other words, he does not have a fairly limited series of responses, some of which may be inappropriate for a particular situation, but he judges his actions in the light of changing circumstances and behaves accordingly.

Perhaps some of my readers have seen bird acts in which parrots are trained to do all sorts of wonderful and unparrotlike things. Many have appeared on television and in the movies, while in a few resort areas there are establishments which have permanent year-round displays of trained birds. There parrots, usually macaws though occasionally cockatoos, are taught to do all sorts of unusual things such as pulling a cart, opening containers, raising the American flag, firing a cannon, riding a bicycle on a tightrope and so on. Other parrots have been taught to tell fortunes by selecting one particular card from a group in return for a food reward. These are only a few of the things which parrots can be taught.

Almost as wonderful are the things which a parrot teaches himself through observation. For example, one particular parrot loved to bathe under the spray from the faucet. He would fly to the sink, squawk until his owner approached and then watch interestedly while the water was turned on. A number of weeks later his owner noticed the parrot tugging at the faucet. Apparently his mind had managed to relate the turning on of the tap to the shower. Eventually he learned to turn on the water whenever he wanted to bathe.

We are including this observation as an example because it contains all the elements necessary to train a parrot. Although in this case the

All parrots love to have their heads scratched. Photo by L. van der Meid.

bird taught himself, the very same principle could be used to teach your bird almost any trick. The principle is simple: the reward must be closely associated with the action which you want the bird to perform. In this particular case, when the faucet was turned the water came gushing forth immediately; the trick was the turning of the faucet, the reward was the shower. An amplification of this principle, the basis for applying it and some specific application are the purposes of this chapter.

Imprinting

Now let us go back to the beginning, that is to the time when you first acquired your pet. Perhaps you have been fortunate enough to acquire a baby bird. Babies are usually taken from the nest prior to their acquiring the power of flight and are hand-reared by a native. If taken early enough, the parrot will forget the members of his avian family and consider himself a human, identifying closely with the person who feeds and cares for him. To understand a little of how this happens, let's digress for a moment for a minor side excursion into a relatively new discipline known as "ethology," the study of animal behavior.

Those of us who have lived on or visited a farm have seen a hen stalking through the barnyard followed by a group of chicks. Usually they tag along behind in a cluster as though attached by strings to the mother figure, and if they scatter in the search for food a gentle "cluck" brings them scurrying back into a tight little ball, again trailing the mother. For the thousands of years that chickens have been domesticated, it has always been taken for granted that chicks follow chickens, ducklings follow ducks, goslings follow geese, cygnets follow swans and so on, or as Aesop put it, "birds of a feather flock together."

No one ever stopped to wonder, at least not out loud, why each followed its own kind! Were chicks *born* with the knowledge of their mother's appearance? When they first ran from the nest, why didn't they follow a bull, a sheep or a dog? Finally, definitive studies were undertaken and an answer was found: chicks follow the first moving object they see after hatching. This process is called "imprinting." Put chicken eggs under a duck, and the newly hatched chicks will then follow the duck foster mother. The period when these attachments are formed is very short, varying from a few minutes or a few hours to a few days. This is known as the "critical period," and, in chicks, it is the first few hours after breaking through the shell.

No one has made a study of the critical period for imprinting in parrots, but we do know that a parrot taken from the nest at a very early age and reared with humans will fancy himself a human; he will not recognize other parrots as being of his own kind, and this lack of recognition extends even to mating. It is highly unusual for a hand-reared parrot reared without the company of others of his kind to successfully mate and raise young. Their refinement is a matter of evolvement as parrots mature in the company of their own kind. If deprived of this cultural experience, they cannot develop the proper behavior.

Of course, the effect of this is to enhance their value as pets. Parrots are gregarious flock birds. They don't like to be alone, but enjoy doing things in the company of others. When taken young enough, the parrot accepts humans as his flock and behaves accordingly. Because of this, taming and training parrots is seldom a problem. As a rule, they make cheerful and willing performers.

However, this does not mean that a bird which is not hand-raised cannot be tamed and trained—far from it. The process involves more time, effort and knowledge, but if you are willing to invest these you can successfully tame and train even the wildest of adults.

In another category is the bird which may have been too old when captured to identify with humans but was still young enough to adjust to his changed surroundings without becoming upset. A bird like this

Parrots are gregarious birds. Photo by L. van der Meid.

will usually stand calmly on the perch as you approach, again eyeing you carefully. If you extend your hand, he will back off; if you persist in your attentions, he will climb the bars of his cage to avoid you. Experienced parrot handlers, when approaching a strange bird, will usually offer not their finger but the back of their clenched fist, fingers down. This is extended slowly, not directly at the bird but at a lower plane on a line with his feet. The fist is gradually brought closer to the bird and, if he shows no signs of panic, moved forward until the knuckles touch just the lower part of his breast. The fingers are then opened slightly and the hand half-rotated so that the edge of the palm presses up and back at the juncture where the legs join the body. Pressure exerted at this point will usually cause the bird to step up on the hand. When approached in this manner birds seldom bite, but the potential danger always exists, so be extremely careful.

If you are not familiar with birds, perhaps a heavy glove is in order. However, most parrot tamers are reluctant to use gloves because some natives when keeping newly captured birds will use heavy gloves and handle the birds roughly during capture and transfer. This causes the birds, which are, as we have said, extremely intelligent, to fear the glove, a fear which is not necessarily transferred to the bare hand. A preferred alternative is to approach the bird with a training stick. This is a piece of doweling 5/8″ to an inch in diameter and about 15 inches long. The stick should never be poked directly at the bird. This will always alarm him. Rather, move it slowly, held crossways to the parrot, again bringing it to the juncture of legs and body, where pressure is exerted back and up to make the parrot step on the "perch."

There are birds in the trade known as "broncs" or "broncos." These are birds that have been captured as adults or have been roughly handled. In any event, they fear and resent men, and any attempt to approach them is met by screams of rage. When cornered, these birds will bite—they can bite severely, so caution is the word.

One note regarding biting: it is rare to find a parrot which will attack without provocation; in my personal experience I have never known one that did. Invariably, a bite is an effort by the parrot to defend him from what he considers an attack or an invasion of his territory—that is, his cage. Even the wildest of parrots will rarely bite if you slowly put your hand into his cage. Rather, he will attempt to avoid your hand and bite only as a last desperate measure when he feels you are about to grab him. Sudden movements may cause a bird to bite, again only because he feels the movement may be directed against himself. So the thing to remember when approaching or moving about a parrot, particularly a strange one, is to move slowly and avoid maneuvering him into such a position that he will feel trapped.

Stick Training

Now let us see how an experienced parrot trainer handles a bird newly arrived from the jungle. Let us assume that this bird was captured as an adult, is thoroughly frightened and confused by the change and is bitterly resentful of his captivity. All his life he has thought of humans as something from which any self-respecting parrot should flee and has depended upon his magnificent powers of flight, as well as his powerful beak, to protect himself. Now he is all alone, confined in a small area and surrounded by the enemy.

Because the parrot is accustomed to perching on a branch, a stick is the logical means for the first approach. Select one of a diameter that he can conveniently grasp; if it is too thin he will have trouble balancing, if

Here, the training stick is used to give a cue. Tapping on the stand causes the cockatoo to raise his wings and "display" like an American eagle. Photo by L. van der Meid.

too thick he may slide off, particularly if it is smooth. For the larger parrots, macaws and cockatoos, a length of 15 inches to two feet and a diameter of 5/8 inch to 1 inch thickness is most suitable.

Strangely enough to us, a parrot in most cases cannot recognize the sex of another parrot by its appearance any more than we can. It is the *behavior* of the other parrot that indicates whether it is male or female, whether it is prepared to challenge, ignore or mate. Aggressive males will face each other directly, whereas a female will turn sideways and bob or bow her head. What does this have to do with training? Very simply this: we make a mistake when we point the stick directly at the bird and move it toward him. It represents a challenge which usually results in his practically falling over backward in his haste to avoid this apparently aggressive enemy. The proper way is to bring the stick sideways toward the bird, but *very, very* slowly. As a rule, it will not panic him, but as it approaches he may try to fend it off with his beak. Try to move it gently out of his grasp and persist in directing—but I repeat, ever so slowly—the side of the stick toward the lower part of his body. If he should scramble away, wait until he calms down for a moment and resume your efforts, but do not remove the stick from the cage no matter how panicky he seems. This is one lesson that he *must* learn.

The normal procedure as mentioned earlier is to bring the stick from the front of the bird to the juncture of leg and body and by pressing upward and backward against his thighs cause him to step up onto the stick. Occasionally you may find a bird that will respond better to a rear approach; that is, the stick is passed around behind his legs and then brought in and pressed forward and upward. The pressure should be firm and steady so that if he doesn't respond promptly he is gradually lifted off his perch. If his head starts darting in all directions and he appears nervous, pause for a few minutes until he calms down; otherwise he'll just flee.

All through the training sessions, talk soothingly to your bird. It doesn't matter what you say—he can't understand the words—but the tone of voice, a calm gentle monotone, will exert a soothing effect and help to familiarize him with you. You can repeat soothingly, "Oh, you're a good boy—yes you are—just step up on it—nobody's going to hurt you," and similar banalities. You can even recite the Declaration of Independence or the Gettysburg Address if you do it soothingly.

Once the bird is up on the stick, reassure him again and move the stick so that now the cage perch is pressing against his leg, and he will step back on the perch. Remove your stick and the first lesson is over. Under no circumstances should you quit without his having stepped on the stick at least once. Regardless of how long it takes and how tiring it is, this minimum step must be accomplished, otherwise you will find training a difficult procedure later on.

After several lessons—by which time he should be stepping promptly on the stick when it is presented to him—prepare two sticks. This time when he steps on the training stick, slowly remove him from the cage. Talk to him quietly while holding him near the cage door and then return him to the cage. Remember that the cage is his security—a sort of avian "security blanket"—so be certain there is nothing in the room to distract or disturb him when he is removed. When he becomes accustomed to going in and out the cage door, walk slowly around the room, always talking to him calmly and reassuringly, and return him to the cage. It will help if you tilt the stick slightly upward and hold your hand fairly high, as a bird always prefers to perch on the highest point. This is when your second stick comes into use. Bring it toward the parrot in the same manner as when you started stick training. Coax and persuade him to step up on this; repeat with the first stick and so on, so that in effect he is climbing a ladder. It will not be long before he steps readily from stick to stick.

This lesson thoroughly learned, present your arm instead of a stick. As a parrot's claws are quite sharp and, particularly when he is nervous, he will tend to clamp down, it is best to have on a thick sleeve. Again repeat the step-to-step process, using your arm as one of the steps. If you slowly lower your arm, the parrot will climb up, endeavoring to

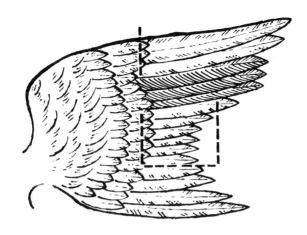

Some people prefer to clip a bird's wings during the training period. The dotted lines show which feathers should be cut away on both wings. After he has molted, the bird will regain the power of flight. Illustrations by M. Youens.

reach the highest point and eventually reach your shoulder, from where he may be removed with a stick. If this phase of the training is done in front of a mirror, it will be easy to locate the bird when it's time for him to step back on the stick.

There is no limit to the number of tricks that a parrot can be taught, although some species, of course, as well as individuals learn to perform better than others. However, in parrot circuses it makes a more colorful show if different birds do different tricks, so the entertainer keeps switching birds each time he wants to demonstrate something new. However, each bird has his "understudy" if for some reason he cannot perform.

In those instances where a bird performs a number of tricks, he knows what is expected of him when he is placed alongside the equipment he is expected to operate. For example, if he is to walk a tightrope the trainer will place him right on the rope. If he is to cling to the handle of an umbrella while it is raised, he is brought alongside the umbrella, and so on. The tricks that a parrot can be taught are limited only by your own imagination, ingenuity and patience.

At first it is best to take your parrot out of the cage only after dark, as parrots have been known to hurt themselves by trying to fly through a closed window. Alternatively, draw the blinds or curtains so that he will not imagine that the glass is a route to freedom. Mirrors should also be covered. This caution, of course, is for those birds that still have their full wings. It is a practice of parrot trappers to cut the wing feathers of the birds to eliminate the possibility of escape, so most parrots imported for sale cannot fly, at least not at first. When they molt the clipped feathers new ones will grow in and the parrot will regain his powers of swift and strong flight.

If something startles your bird while he is out of the cage, the chances are he will jump off the stick. If he can fly he will undoubtedly circle the room several times in a panic. If his wings have been clipped he will flutter to the floor. In either case he will be quite upset. Wait calmly until he has settled down and then approach him slowly with a stick while talking soothingly. Each time he runs or flies away, wait for him to settle down and try again. If circumstances demand that you catch him without delay toss a large beach towel, a light blanket or even a coat over him and pick him up in that. Do not try to catch him with your hands, as a frightened parrot will bite.

When these lessons are thoroughly learned, and only then, use your hand instead of the stick to lift him. If he shows nervousness, backs off or squawks when you use your hand, continue the stick and arm training for a while longer and try again. Eventually he will step right up on your hand when it is presented to him. You can then try removing him from the cage on your hand instead of with a stick. By this time your parrot will be so accustomed to you and the sound of your voice that he will be amenable to further training.

Head Scratching

Most parrots love to have their heads scratched, but a premature attempt to do so will only alarm the bird. In nature, danger comes from overhead, and therefore a parrot suspects anything which approaches above his line of vision. Use a rubber-tipped pencil and, with the bird on his stick, bring the pencil toward his cheek. If you move slowly he will allow you to gently rub the side of his head around the eye. Gradually extend this area of rubbing until you are scratching the back of his head, a process which most parrots enjoy so much that they will bow their heads to facilitate the rubbing. In a matter of time you can substitute your finger for the pencil.

So far we have discussed everything in terms of gaining the bird's confidence, familiarizing him with you and teaching him to respond to the movements of the sticks, a process which may take days, weeks or, in the case of a really suspicious bird, several months. At this point you will have a thoroughly responsive pet, and if you want to go further with his training it is only a matter of knowledge and an understanding of the principles involved.

Tricks

All animals learn by association. The Russian physiologist Ivan Pavlov rang a bell each time he fed his dogs. After a number of trials he found that the dogs would salivate at the ringing of the bell in anticipation of the meal. In other words, he had taught them to associate a bell with food. For a reward to be effective it must be closely associated with the action performed, so that the bird can learn that the reward comes as a result of his action. While parrots are undoubtedly among the most intelligent, if not the most intelligent of birds, there is a limit to their reasoning ability and they are easily distracted. Therefore, we must select some method of directing their attention to the proper performance immediately when it is done. For this purpose professional trainers have found a small cricket or snapper most suitable. This is the children's toy which makes a click something like a castanet when the metal tongue is pressed. A suitable reward is also required, and for parrots the most effective is raw peanuts. A supply of these should be prepared beforehand by removing the shells and cutting the kernel into quarters.

While food is normally kept in front of a parrot at all times, in preparation for training remove the food cup several hours earlier. It is amazing to find how delicately a parrot can manipulate his strong beak

This well-trained Moluccan cockatoo responds to the commands of its owner and trainer. However, it is reported to get agitated by photographers that come too close. Photo by K. Donnelly.

Each parrot selects a perch or area to be his own favorite spot, and he resents intruders. Photo by L. van der Meid.

to pick up even the smallest particles. Once your bird is accustomed to being handled, try hand-feeding him. Start by offering him a whole peanut with one hand while holding the snapper in the other. As he takes the peanut, click the snapper. From whole peanuts, you can progress to giving him kernels, half-kernels and finally quarter-kernels, but each time you give him the food from your hand snap the cricket. It will not take too long before he will associate the sound of the cricket with the food.

Hauling a Bucket

One of the easiest tricks to teach a parrot is to haul up a bucket or pot suspended from a chain. Remove his food for several hours (two or three) and hang a small pot on a fine-link chain 18 inches to two feet below his perch. Put several hulled peanuts in the pot. By tapping the pot with your finger you can draw his attention to it and then lift the chain several times with your fingers, letting it drop each time. When he shows an interest in the chain by picking at it, snap the cricket and give him a small piece of peanut. This will encourage him to continue his interest in the chain. The first few times he picks up the chain reward him, but then discontinue the rewards until he learns to hold the chain under his foot, or he will continually drop the bucket in expectation of the reward. It is now a matter of timing to encourage him, by the use of the cricket, to continue picking the chain up until he can reach the reward. It is almost like the game of "hot and cold." The sound of the cricket coming directly, in fact almost coinciding, with the action tells him when he is doing the right thing.

Other tricks such as hauling up the American flag can be taught the same way. It is also a matter of directing his attention to the rope or string which raises the flag. When he starts to mouth it, snap the cricket and give him his reward. Continue this until he learns to pull at the string and raise the flag to the top.

To summarize: we draw his attention to the object which we want him to interest himself in. We reward his preliminary actions with a snap of the cricket and a quarter peanut, but discontinue rewarding the preliminary steps until he has progressed to the next stage. We do this successively until he has completed the training.

Again, the same method can be used to call a bird to you. Stand a short distance away from a hungry bird, offer him food and, when he cranes or inclines toward you, snap your cricket. Each time withhold the rewards by degrees until he has to fly to you to receive his food.

Hand-training the Smaller Parrots and Parakeets

It is remarkable how quickly the newly captured adults of most of the smaller species of parrots and parakeets can be hand-tamed. This, I feel, is due in large part to their unique intelligence which enables them to evaluate a situation and to respond to it on a practical basis.

While it is both possible and practical to hand-train smaller birds in the same way as the larger ones, their training can be done in a much simpler and less time-consuming manner. First of all, the wings must be clipped. Many of the birds, particularly those from South America, arrive with the wings already cut. The natives do this because they are afraid that the birds will escape from the crude cages in which they are kept before they are taken to market.

Wearing a pair of leather gloves to avoid being bitten, grasp the bird by the back, holding his wings against his body. The basic position is with the bird's head pointing in the direction of your thumb, with the thumb itself holding the left wing in place, while the other four fingers are curled around the right wing. The back of the bird fits in the palm of your hand. Set the bird on the extended forefinger of your left hand and hold him there until he has firmly grasped your finger with his claws. The chances are that as soon as he feels your grip relax, he will jump off. This is perfectly normal, so don't be discouraged. Recapture the bird (this is best done in a room without a lot of furniture that he can scuttle under) and replace him on your finger.

Repeat this procedure every time he jumps off. It is amazing how soon he will just stand there and squawk. When he reaches this stage, replace him in his cage by extending the hand on which he is standing through the cage door and moving him up against a perch onto which he can step. Probably, when he is taken out again for his next lesson, he will resume the jumping and fleeing, but it will require less time before he decides to stay on your finger. Sometimes two or three lessons are enough to finger-train him; rarely does it require more than six. Lessons can be given two or three times a day.

When he has learned to remain on your finger, extend the finger of the other hand so that it presses against the juncture of legs and body. Press slowly but firmly against this point until he steps up on the finger and continue with finger-training in the same way as stick-training.

The gloves can be discarded after the first few lessons. In fact, it will probably not be necessary to wear a glove on the left hand, as I have never known a parrot to bend over and bite the hand on which he was set. However, if you are nervous and unused to parrots, perhaps it is best to wear one, at least in the beginning.

It is clear that this amazon parrot trusts its trainer. Photo by Dr. Herbert R. Axelrod.

VIII   Teaching Your Parrot to Talk

It is very difficult, but not impossible, to teach a parrot to talk if he has not first been hand-tamed, so I will assume that you have followed the suggestions given in the previous chapter on taming and that your pet is now ready for his next step.

As I have already pointed out, some species of parrots are, of course, more skillful at talking than others. All members of the family will learn to talk if raised from the nest or tamed when very young, but there is a great deal of difference in the learning ability of the individual. However, with perseverance almost any parrot, even an older one, can be taught to mimic to some degree.

Before a bird will begin to talk, he must feel comfortable and relaxed in the presence of his trainer and he should never be frightened by other pets, boisterous children or sudden noises and abrupt movements. If a bird becomes timorous and fearful in the beginning, weeks of hard work will be needed to regain his lost confidence. This is why a new arrival should be placed where he can observe people and yet be far enough away not to be alarmed by the normal bustle of the household.

On the other hand, one cannot expect a parrot to talk if he is never let out of his cage, just fed and watered regularly but ignored for the rest of the day. Attention and kindness—so that the bird will come to love and trust you—are equally essential ingredients.

Good Talkers

Most parrot keepers agree that the African grey is one of the best talkers of them all. Even untamed greys have been known to mimic human speech. They seem to have an almost uncanny human reasoning power in their ability to fit the word to the action.

The blue-fronted amazon is good, too. I have heard of one who repeated the Lord's Prayer from beginning to end without a mistake. The Mexican red-heads I have known were all fair talkers. So too are the yellow-napes and the Panama greens, although I must admit of knowing one Panama who never learned to say more than his own name. A Mexican double-yellow started to talk when four months old and at seven months was singing, laughing and able to whistle a tune without missing a note.

Sad to say, though, among the beautiful cockatoos that I have known, including the sulphur-crested, both large and small, and the Leadbeater's, I have never heard more than three words. But at the other end of the scale I have had budgerigars (shell parakeets) that could chatter entire sentences. I myself have not had too much luck with cockatiels, but I know many people who have. With this species the cock learns better than the hen. The Indian ring-neck parakeet is a beautiful bird and a fair talker, and yet an Alexandrine I know has never uttered a word.

Intelligence

Always remember that a talking bird is a mimic; he does not reason. He repeats by rote words and sentences he has been taught or ones that he has overheard. What sometimes appears to be thinking, as when a bird answers a question, is simply a matter of word association, while a

A pair of cockatiels (male, right). Some people believe that the male learns to talk more readily, but either sex will, with very little training, learn to whistle a tune. Photo by H. Müller.

good-morning greeting or a good-night farewell appropriately delivered is merely time association.

Baron Cuvier, a French zoologist (1769-1852), discusses the subject of parrot intelligence most interestingly in his best-known work, *The Animal Kingdom:*

> We must not consider the articulated voice of the parrot as a proof of the superiority of his intelligence over that of other animals, or of its analogy with our own. It is certainly true that the parrot exhibits the most perfect brain to be found among any of the feathered race—but as to the intelligence of the bird, compared with ours, it can only be considered that there is a point of contact between them, as it were, but no resemblance. The parrot's imitation seems purely mechanical; it articulates words indeed, but this cannot be considered a true language. He does not comprehend their significance, and though he may repeat them on certain occasions because he has learned them, he sees no reason for doing so like man.

He utters, indifferently, a prayer or an insult, and those involuntary substitutions, which really prove his want of intelligence, pass, with unreflecting persons, for a mark of wit, of irony, or of some other quality of mind of which the animal is utterly destitute.

Many stories have been told, and repeated *usque ad nauseam,* of the marvelous deeds of these birds supposed to be consequent on their mental faculties; indeed, most persons are in possession of anecdotes, more or less wonderful, of particular individuals, which have fallen under their own observation, or that of their friends—anecdotes, which too often increase by repetition, till the true extent and character of the original facts is lost.

Parrots will certainly sometimes repeat a word or a sentence, which circumstances may render particularly apt and applicable, as monkeys will sometimes use a gesture or an action strikingly human in its appearance; but a very slight acquaintance with these animals will convince any reasonable person that these imitative or mechanical qualities are not to be attributed to superior reason or sagacity; and, as much has been already said upon the subject, we shall not subjoin any repetition of thrice-told tales which, however amusing, may be considered as destitute of instruction, and of equivocal veracity.

Sex

In my opinion, the sex of the bird has no bearing whatsoever on its ability to imitate. In a great many cases the owner is not even aware of the sex of his pet. Many times has the wrong name been used until "Harry" suddenly lays an egg!

As to the sex of the trainer, this is a different matter. All are agreed that women and children make the best speech trainers. There is something in their voice that has a more soothing effect on birds, and the pitch and tone are closer to the bird's own and therefore easier to imitate. Interesting too is the observation that a male parrot usually prefers women, and a female, men.

Under Cover

Many trainers believe that a bird learns to talk more quickly if the cage is covered during the training session. I personally have found no evidence for this. I feel that the bird likes to see as well as hear his trainer. However, there are many who disagree with me, and if you should discover that your bird does learn faster when covered or when you remain out of sight, by all means use this method. Sometimes just covering the back and two sides of the cage increases the bird's concentration.

Attention

Particularly in the beginning, when the bird is still learning, his attention should be completely concentrated on the trainer, so no toys or other distractions like a mirror should be left in the cage. Do not try to teach two birds at a time or even keep them both in the same room during training sessions. They will imitate each other, not you.

Improprieties

While it sometimes seems like fun to teach vulgar words and oaths, one should always bear in mind that the bird may utter them at an inappropriate moment. Talking birds seem to pick up "swear words" quite readily; this is probably because such expressions are sharp and distinct, and usually uttered with explosive force.

A "Secret" Method

Here is a summary of what a very accomplished bird trainer told me about her method. To begin with, she pointed out, we must remember that teaching parrots to talk only *seems* to be a slow process. We should realize that it takes a child nearly two years before he does much talking. So why should we be so impatient with a bird?

Many people have asked her about her method, thinking perhaps she had found some great secret. "The secret," she insists, "is patience and perseverance—and nothing else!"

She believes that birds learn best between seven and nine o'clock in the morning and between seven and nine in the evening, and that they also talk more during these two periods. She thinks the bird learns faster if he does not watch you during the lesson and that he pays closer attention if you remain just out of his sight range.

She then says clearly whatever word or phrase that she wishes the bird to learn, and always pauses between each repetition for it to sink in. She never utters another expression during the entire period. She is particularly careful not to speak to a dog or cat or to any person who might be in the house. She repeats the chosen phrase for at least a quarter of an hour, morning and evening. She then leaves the bird alone, without even a word of endearment or parting, to think over what he has just heard. Otherwise, she points out, it is quite possible that an extraneous interjection may be jumbled into the expression you are trying to teach.

Supplement the regular training sessions by using the same word or phrase whenever you are in the room with the parrot, and especially when you greet him in the morning and after you have turned out the light at night.

If a new parrot does not begin to talk after a reasonable time, try training him in a darkened room twice each day for a half hour. It is better to sit where the parrot can hear but not see you. Many trainers have reported that, with their patience exhausted, they gave up regular training only to overhear the bird some time later uttering clearly the word or phrase that they had tried for so long to teach.

It goes without saying that a bird should never be punished for stubbornly refusing to repeat the word or phrase you are trying to teach him. Punishment will only make things worse. Parrots have better memories than elephants and never forgive or forget what they consider a wrong.

Word and Time Association

Perhaps you would like to have your bird show off by answering questions. "Who's the greatest?" perhaps, to have the bird reply, "I am!" Start by teaching the answer first; in this case, "I am!" When the bird has learned the answer, teach the question *and* the answer. Then when he hears you say "Who's the greatest?" he will complete it with "I am!" He will, of course, eventually learn to repeat both question and answer, sometimes together, sometimes interchangeably, but this too can be amusing.

Parrots appear to have a great sense of time and occasion. When and where you teach the desired expression has a great bearing on its time of repetition. A "Good morning" taught in the morning will almost always be uttered only in the morning, and a "Good night" taught in the evening will be repeated only then. If the bird learns the name of food as it is being fed, he will be inclined to repeat that name only when he sees the food. And they quickly learn the names of the members of the family and of other pets and almost always use them correctly.

The Reward Method

While I am of the opinion that a parrot must first be hand-tamed before he will begin to speak, there are those who believe that taming and talk-training can go hand in hand. They remove all food and water from the cage in the afternoon (or offer none at all except during the training session) and then next morning feed and water the untamed bird entirely by hand; as they do so they utter the word or phrase they want the bird to learn.

For example, they say "Good morning" and then present a tasty seed or nut, then more food with a "Good morning" and so on repeatedly. The adherents to this "reward" theory believe that by identifying the

Prior to training for special tricks or for talking, a parrot can become accustomed to accepting food from the hand. Photo by Dr. H. R. Axelrod.

phrase with the food, the word becomes a pleasing sound, one that the bird welcomes. Then later on, when the bird is alone, he will have been conditioned into uttering the expression to attract attention—and, of course, if he does so, he should be rewarded immediately with food and soothing compliments. Once the bird repeats the phrase, he should of course never be rewarded until after the phrase has been uttered. Then lessons on a new phrase can begin.

As the bird becomes more and more tame he will become more and more attached to his trainer and the reward will then be the trainer's mere presence. The bird will talk to bring the trainer to him, remain silent while the trainer is present and resume talking if the trainer starts to leave.

Professor O. H. Mowrer of Harvard University has an amusing story along this line. His parrot, a Mexican red-head, was set in his cage out of doors in the sun. The neighbor's children came to visit him. They tried to get the bird to talk but he would not utter a sound. The children, finally tiring of the one-sided conversation, started to leave. Immediately the parrot called out sharply, "Don't go!" Mowrer declares that no attempt had ever been made to teach him this expression, and that only once afterward was he ever heard to use it again. It would appear that as long as the children were there entertaining *him,* the parrot saw no reason to entertain *them.*

I agree with Professor Mowrer that a bird likes to see and hear his trainer, but that if he can see him, it is not so important to hear him. This is why, he believes, the "covering the cage" approach sometimes succeeds in talk-training when all else fails. In a covered cage, the bird does not know that the trainer is still present until he hears his voice. The bird will talk to get the trainer to talk to reassure him of his presence.

Many owners never realize their pet's full talking potential. When their bird has learned a few words or phrases, they abandon all further training. This is a mistake. The most difficult teaching period is the one before the bird utters his first word. After that it is all clear sailing, but still a certain amount of concentrated effort is required, and the phrases that have been learned should constantly be reviewed.

Recordings

There are on the market a number of phonograph records that can be used for teaching a parrot to talk. If you do not have the time or patience to teach the bird yourself, these records can be very helpful. But perhaps an even better idea, if you have a tape recorder, is to tape one of your own training sessions and then repeatedly play it back to the bird while you go about your household duties, because a parrot mimics not just the words but also the tone of voice and the inflection. It is flattering to hear your own voice repeated.

Mimicry is not just limited to words. A parrot will sing or whistle a tune, do bird calls, bark like a dog or meow like a cat. Any noise which he hears often enough to be impressed on his memory will be repeated eventually, even the sound of inanimate objects like the car horn, a door slamming or a motor.

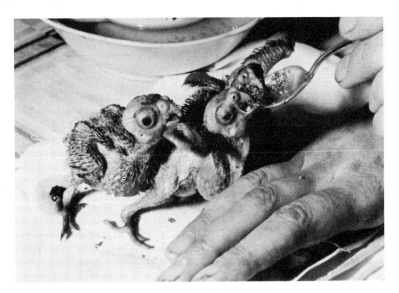

Baby cockatiels being hand-fed. Photo by H. Müller.

Part II Parrots in General

I Breeding

At one time the breeding of parrots, with the exception of the common budgerigars, was thought to be so difficult that it could not be attempted by amateurs. Progress has helped to solve this problem by producing new materials which have contributed considerably to making cage and aviary accommodations much more efficient and, above all, more sanitary and antiseptic. With a little ingenuity it is possible to build well-designed breeding aviaries or to adapt older buildings for this purpose.

When breeding parrots, it must be kept in mind that most if not all species are extremely antagonistic during their mating period. They resent the presence of any other bird except their mate, and frequently even mating pairs are unsympathetic. This is why, if you expect a pair to mate, the two birds must be housed in a separate aviary. It is wiser, too, to set up the nesting boxes in the flight rather than in a shelter, as the fledgling birds will need all the air and bright sunlight that they can get.

It should also be remembered that almost no members of the parrot family will mate if they are not content. Their living conditions must be exemplary. Their diet must be exactly right, their health perfect. Most of the larger parrots do not fully mature until they are several years old; this also applies to the larger parakeets and conures. The smaller species, with their much shorter life spans, usually come into maturity somewhat earlier. But in almost every case, patience and an understanding of the particular species' nesting needs are necessary if the attempt is not to end in disappointment.

However, some of the larger parrots have been known to breed in strange places and rear their young most successfully. In one case a pair of African grays—a four-year-old hen and a twelve-year-old cock—nested in an oak chest full of old books stored in an attic. The birds were allowed the attic as a playroom, but one day they decided it was time to give up playing and settle down to the real business of raising a family. Their first nest produced two chicks, and in subsequent years they had other nests ranging from one to four babies.

Another owner had a pair that seemed anxious to breed. Being short of space, he fenced in his kitchen table with chain link fencing and gave the birds a length of rotting wood. In due time the hen laid four eggs in a hollow she scooped out of the log, and all four eggs hatched, although only three chicks were reared.

Several cases have been reported of African greys nesting in large cages made of packing cases. When wooden cages are used it is necessary to cover the outside of the woodwork with heavy-gauge wire netting because it doesn't take long for a nesting hen to gnaw through a one-inch board.

Except for the lovebirds and quaker parakeets, parrots need no nesting material; they prefer to lay their two or more white eggs in the hollows of decaying tree trunks or in man-made boxes that simulate these natural nesting places. The nest should not be too large, just large enough to house the mother and the one to six fledglings, while the entrance hole should be just big enough for the parents to squeeze through.

The eggs of the large species need approximately one month to hatch, those of the small about three weeks.

Sexing

With many species it is difficult to sex the birds. There are in some varieties certain indications such as size of head and beak or feather and bone formation. Perhaps the best guide to sexing similarly colored birds is their behavior when they are in full breeding condition. Then the cock birds usually become noisy and perform various dance-like antics while the hen birds turn coy and start searching for a nesting place. In our catalog on the various species the visible sexual differences are described if they are known to the writer.

Macaws, Cockatoos and Large Parrots

These birds are not easy to breed in captivity, and to breed them specific knowledge of their nesting habits is necessary—knowlege that can only come from experience. First of all, a spacious aviary and flight for *each* mating pair is necessary—this in itself is a large order. It can, of course, be built along the lines given in my chapter on aviary construction, but it should be very large—the larger the better—and it cannot house more than the two birds being bred.

In the wild these birds nest in hollow trees, enlarging the holes with their beaks. The larger birds usually lay two eggs in a clutch, the smaller ones three or four. The nests are not lined, the hen laying her eggs on the rotting wood. In the aviary, a hollow log will have to be provided. It should stand upright with a hole at the top and be hollow for several feet down. Sometimes a hollow tree trunk can be planted in the flight. Sawing it in transverse sections and reassembling it at the nesting site makes it easier to transport. A barrel with a hole in the top just large enough for them to enter will also serve. Put a concave block of old wood on the bottom to keep the eggs from rolling and a wire mesh "ladder" inside the barrel leading down from the hole.

The incubation period lasts about a month, depending on the species. Both parents feed the nestlings.

Cockatiels

These birds are among the easiest to breed. The cock should always be older than the hen, and both birds should be at least six months old, preferably a year, before they are bred. Although it is possible to breed cockatiels in indoor cages, an outdoor flight will prove much more successful. Only one pair should be kept in the enclosure.

Commercially made nest boxes are available. They should be attached near the roof or on top of a pole. A nest box should be at least 18 inches long, 15 inches wide and 12 inches high. A three-inch hole serves for the entrance, with a six-inch perch placed below it. A block of wood with a gouged-out depression is placed inside the box. No nesting material is needed.

Cockatiels lay from five to eight eggs that require about three weeks for incubation. The eggs are incubated during the day by the cock and by the hen at night. It is reported that even if the hen dies, the cock will never leave his roosting place at the entrance of the nest hole to sit on the eggs at night, so the eggs also die.

Small Parakeets and Lovebirds

Commercially manufactured budgerigar nesting boxes are the best to use for breeding the smallest parakeets and parrotlets, and they can even be used for the African lovebirds if the entrance hole is enlarged. Those boxes that include inspection doors are the most practical.

Generally speaking, the clutches of eggs range from two to six, are white in color and are roundish in shape. An egg starts incubating as soon as it is laid; as eggs are laid one at a time over a period of days, there is a difference in the growth of babies in each clutch. The period of incubation varies with each group, ranging from 20 to 25 days. In some species both sexes share in the incubation and in others it is solely the duty of the hen, although in all cases both birds help to feed the chicks.

For the first days of their lives the young are fed on food that is predigested and regurgitated by the parents directly into the babies' mouths. Then as they get older they are fed on seed direct from the crops of their parents.

The smaller members of the family seem to breed better in captivity than do most of their larger relatives. In addition to the pure-bred birds, it is not unusual for related species to hybridize; some beautifully colored examples of hybrids have been produced.

Some of the parakeets, such as the red-rumped, ring-necked and Bourke's, and cockatiels have become more or less domesticated, and other colored phases of these birds are now being bred. Special types of nesting boxes are sold for these species.

Breeders often band the young of the smaller birds for identification, and some nesting boxes have hinged inspection doors which make this banding easier. There is much to be said for the use of bands, as they enable breeders to keep track of their stock. These bands help considerably when planning matings as they prevent the use of too closely related birds for breeding purposes. It is advantageous if the breeder bands all stock birds, even adults. Bands can be obtained from manufacturers whose advertisements will be found in the cage bird journals.

Lovebirds

Members of the lovebird group are usually free-breeders in captivity, and this characteristic has led to the production of several new color varieties. An interesting thing about this group is that although they nest in boxes, they line their nests with bark and coarse grass. Their nesting boxes are similar to those sold for budgerigars but they should be made slightly deeper to accommodate their special nesting habits. Like the budgerigar, lovebirds will raise several broods a year. In most

Unusual among parrot family birds, lovebirds fill their nesting cavities with straw and grasses. This is a nest of a masked lovebird with the cover removed. Photo by H. Muller.

cases they make really first-class parents. For this reason they make good birds for the beginning breeder.

Conures, Small Parrots and Large Parakeets

These medium sized birds should have nest boxes at least 16 inches long, 8 inches deep and 6 inches high. As with the larger parrots and macaws, they should be housed only in mating pairs.

A tree trunk can be simulated by a "grandfather clock" type of nest box. This is a tall narrow box about the size of the pendulum case of a grandfather clock and at least seven feet high. The bottom is covered with fine wire mesh to keep out rodents and the box is filled to whatever depth from the entrance the particular species requires. Peat moss topped by a layer of decayed wood serves as the nest. This filling, in most cases, rises to within 18 inches of the entrance hole at the top. The interior should be made climbable by tacking a strip of wire netting to the side extending from the hole to the layer of moss. Some species require a longer "climb-down" than others.

A pair of eastern rosellas with a simulated "hollow log" in which to breed. Photo by H. Müller.

Some species, like the Alexandrine, prefer to nest sideways, and for them a small keg will serve as a nest. It is hung high in the flight horizontally, not vertically, with a hole drilled in what was formerly the keg's lid. A little sawdust can be placed on the concave "floor" to keep the eggs from rolling, but no other nesting material is needed.

Lories and Lorikeets

Although several species of lories and lorikeets are kept in captivity, fanciers do not always realize that these nectar-feeding birds are relatively easy to breed and are more amenable to confined quarters than some of the seed-eating parrots. Their beautiful rich colors make them desirable as pets and aviary birds, but their drawback is their messy feeding which requires more time to be devoted to keeping them and their cages clean. Most species nest well in the usual parakeet nest box, but some drainage holes are needed at the bottom, as well as a good layer of peat moss or cat litter to absorb the surplus moisture from their copious droppings.

Quaker Parakeets

These birds breed reasonably well in captivity. In fact, I know several pairs of quakers kept in the Whipsnade Zoological Gardens in England which breed at liberty. Quakers differ from all other parrots in that they build nests that are strong, well-constructed structures woven with twigs. From four to six eggs are usually laid; the incubation period is 31 days. Obviously they will breed only in an aviary. A big heap of sticks and twigs must be provided and a platform of tree branches erected on which they can build the nest.

Amazons

As far as I can find in the records, there have been relatively few attempts to breed any of the amazon parrots in captivity. Those efforts that have been made have seldom been successful beyond producing eggs. Edward Boosey, an English breeder, reported success with blue-fronted and Cuban amazons. He used a "grandfather clock" kind of nesting box.

Although there are undoubtedly more amazons kept in captivity than other large parrots, the few breeding attempts may be due to the fact that they are nearly always kept as household pets. When parrots are tamed as pets they tend to become more attached to human beings than to their own kind, and before very long they forget about breeding.

I do think that if true pairs of amazons, not pets, were given the chance to breed in well-constructed aviaries with the correct kind of nesting sites, they would go to nest and rear young. The following story, I believe, supports this statement.

Some years ago a European dealer in birds found in a consignment of South American parrots some twenty blue-fronted amazons. The feathers of two of them were badly spoiled on the sea voyage. These two he put in one of his parrot aviaries to allow them to molt and regrow new plumage. This happened in April.

During the summer months the birds came under the care of one of his helpers. The floor of the aviary was covered with grass which had grown long and thick in places. The birds spent a lot of time on this grassy floor and seemed to derive a great deal of benefit from what they found to eat, judging by the fine way their new feathers grew.

One day toward the end of September the helper could see only one of the two blue-fronts and became rather perturbed, fearing that one had escaped, as by this time they both could fly very well. A search revealed nothing. Then the dreadful thought crossed the helper's mind that the missing bird was perhaps ill or even dead somewhere in the long grass.

The flight, which was some 12 feet wide by 15 feet long, was carefully searched. When the assistant approached an overgrown area he was suddenly startled by a hissing, growling noise, and there at his feet was the missing bird. She was crouched, with feathers raised, uttering fearful noises over three white oval eggs. She had dug out a hollow under the roots of a matted grass clump to serve as a nest and had nearly completed her clutch.

The owner on his return was delighted over what had taken place and decided at once to leave the birds in peace, hoping that they would hatch out the eggs. However, this was not to be, as it would be nearly November before they were due to hatch, and the weather was cold and wet. After a very cold night the hen decided that she could no longer continue with her maternal duties, and she reluctantly left the eggs. These were examined and were all found to contain developing chicks—so near and yet not near enough!

The birds were removed to winter quarters and in the following spring were sold to an amateur bird breeder. They were duly installed in an aviary similar to the original one and soon settled down. I do not know the final outcome, but the last I heard was that the pair had made no further attempt at breeding. Their first experience with winter weather must have made them reconsider.

Infertile Eggs

A common question frequently asked of all bird breeders is whether hens lay eggs if they have not "known" a male. The answer is, of course, yes. The formation of eggs in birds is akin to the periodic menstruation of mammals, and as we all know, mammals have these periods regularly without necessarily giving birth. To give birth, they must first be fertilized by a male. And, of course, if a bird is to lay a *fertile* egg she too must be impregnated by a male. His sperms are deposited in her cloaca. They then travel up the oviduct into an area where they penetrate the cell membranes of the ova, fertilizing them. In later stages, layers of albumin and shell are gradually built up around the egg before it is laid.

But many times the hen is stimulated to form an egg without having been fertilized. This can happen when union with the male is broken off before the sperms are correctly deposited, or it can happen when a tame female parrot becomes overexcited by her keeper's attentions. Frequently, if there are no males present, two females will pair off and lay eggs (infertile, obviously). And if there are no females present, two males have been known to team up and go to nest.

Upon exposure to the air the down feathers fluff out as seen in these cockatiel hatchlings. Photo by H. V. Lacey.

II   Anatomy and Physiology

Perhaps it will be of interest to my readers to learn something of their pet's anatomical structure and physiology. This book is not intended as a textbook on ornithology, and no attempt has been made to treat this subject other than cursorily, with the thought that it might enable some of my readers to utilize this knowledge for their pet's proper maintenance.

Skeletal Structure

The bone structure of all birds is light, strong and resilient, and we find this no less true of the parrots and their kin. If the bones are examined carefully, it will be seen that while they are apparently fragile they are strongly constructed and hollow. This is nature's way of giving strength while reducing weight. After all, the less he must lift the easier it is for a bird to fly. Bones are built of various mineral elements, principally calcium, and it is essential that these elements be included in the bird's diet.

Wings

Wings, of course, differ in structure according to the species. For instance, the parakeets are birds of swift flight; consequently they have tapering wings, long tails and strong muscles, while some of the larger parrots, not given to flying great distances in the wild, have shorter and rounder wings and tails. But all members of the order can fly. There is no evidence that any of them, even in ages past, ever lost the power of flight—that is, there are no naturally grounded birds in the family (like the ostrich or rhea), although the rare ground parakeet does spend a lot of time on the ground, taking wing only when it's frightened.

A bird's wing is like a modified human arm. I realize that you cannot examine the bones of a parrot's wing too closely, but the bones of a chicken wing are much the same and readily available. You will find that the "upper arm" is a large bone attached by a ball-and-socket joint to the shoulder. The "lower arm" has two bones like man's. The end structure is analogous to the hand. There is a wrist joint and the primitive bone structure of a thumb and two fingers.

The shoulder blades are imbedded in the muscles of the bird's back. The collar bone (what we call the wishbone) merges in front of the breastbone, forming a V. What zoologists call the coracoids brace the shoulder against the breastbone. While the bones are light, the muscles that power the wings are incredibly strong. For a man to be able to fly like a bird he would have to have wings each about 70 feet long and the strength to beat them in the air about 500 times a minute.

Feathers

Although it is hard to believe, feathers are akin to fish scales and are made up of pretty much the same proteinaceous material, which is known as keratin. The beak and claws consist of the same fibrous tissue. Developing from follicles in the skin, feathers grow only in certain areas, but from there they spread out to cover all the bare parts. Feathers are really a marvelous invention. Light but strong, they insulate a bird from heat and cold, help protect him from his enemies, shield him from rain and sun and beautify him.

There are several types of feathers. *Down* forms the plumage of the nestlings. Then there are hairlike feathers with a tufted end known as *filoplumes*. These are usually concealed by the *contour* feathers and help to insulate the bird. Contour feathers give the bird its streamlined shape and provide the basic coloration. *Quill* feathers grow in the wings and tail; these are, of course, necessary to flight. *Powder down* consists of a patch of soft feathery material that gives off tiny particles of a dusty substance used by some parrots to clean their feathers.

A quill feather is the easiest to examine. The central axis (although it is a little off center) is known as the rachis (pronounced ray-kiss). The lower, hollow part of the rachis is known as the calamus or quill. At its base is an opening through which the growing feather is nourished. From the rachis the feather fans out in a flat vane that is wider on one side than the other. The rays are known as barbs. Each of these is like another tiny feather, and they are laced together by interlocking hooks. Sometimes a feather is "split" so these tiny hooks come apart, but the bird can lock them again by preening and shaking its feathers.

At the base of the tail on most species there is an oil gland. The bird uses its beak to spread oil from this gland into its feathers to make them waterproof.

Molting

All of the feathers are shed at least once a year, sometimes even more often under captive conditions. This molt is usually keyed to the increase in sunlight as the days lengthen in summer. Near the equator, where the length of the day is constant all year round, the molt is probably triggered by the rainy season. The new feathers grow from the follicles of the old ones. This is why it is wise to pull out a badly broken feather to give the new one a chance to start growing immediately. Since this is momentarily painful, hold the feather base firmly and give one quick jerk. Otherwise you must wait until the stump is molted. We must remember that a parrot's feathers are loosely affixed to his body, particularly his tail feathers. An enemy seizing him is often left with just a mouthful of feathers while the intended victims flies off unharmed. The missing feathers will soon grow back.

Respiration

The lungs lie in the back against the ribs and are relatively small. A rapid rate of breathing fills them often. Their capacity is increased by a series of air sacs which extend out from them. These are believed to assist in heat elimination. Birds have no sweat glands in the skin to cool them when they are warm. Evaporation of liquid, for its cooling effect, takes place in the throat and air sacs. They pant like dogs when resting in the hot sun. They will also hold their wings away from their body to reduce the heat. Parrots react quickly to impure air, immediately showing their distress.

Because of the muscular strain imposed by flight, a bird's metabolism and temperature are quite high. Most birds' temperatures range from 105°F to 108°F, and temperatures as high as 116°F have been recorded. This is why a bird feels warm to the touch. Their pulse rate is also very rapid, at least twice that of a human.

Beak

The most outstanding feature of the members of the parrot family is, of course, their beak, which is hooked like those of the birds of prey although none of the parrots are carnivorous. The upper mandible of almost all other birds is fixed to the skull, while the same structure in parrots is hinged and movable. Beaks are controlled by extremely strong muscles. It is nothing for some parrots to gnaw through inch-thick wood. Since both the upper and lower mandibles are movable, the birds get a tremendous purchase when biting. They also use their beaks to help them climb.

Beaks are made of the same horn-like material (keratin) as are the claws and feathers and continue growing throughout the bird's life. In the wild they are kept worn down by the constant search for food. In captivity they must in some cases be trimmed.

Beak color varies according to the species and, in some species, according to sex. While black or dark beaks appear stronger than those that are red or flesh-colored, in actual fact there is no difference whatsoever in their strength.

The brush-tongued nectar- and fruit-feeding species do not have such powerful beaks as do the seed-eating parrots; nevertheless, their beaks are relatively strong and are used effectively for protection and for carving out and trimming their nesting places.

Smell

This is a moot question, but observation has led me to the conclusion that the vast majority of birds (including the parrot family) have little or no real sense of smell. It was once thought that birds of prey and carrion eaters must have a strong sense of smell to guide them to their food, but experiments to prove this have never been conclusive. It is most probably their acute eyesight that guides them to their food.

The nostrils are invariably situated just above the top of the beak and are usually surrounded by a small area devoid of feathers that is known as the cere. This characteristic is more noticeable in some species than in others. With budgerigars, it is a distinctive feature that serves to differentiate the sexes. In some of the large parrots there is only a comparatively small area of bare skin around the nostrils; in others it extends high up the face.

While their sense of smell is probably inferior to a human's, parrots are much more susceptible to gas in the air. A gas leak which might cause only minor discomfort to a human could kill a bird.

Taste

Like the sense of smell, the sense of taste is not well-developed. We must remember that birds bolt their food whole, without chewing, so there is little need for taste in the sense that we know it. I have found that parrots undoubtedly taste strong spices and kindred flavors in their food. On the other hand, one experimenter tells of feeding a parrot bits of bread dipped in quinine, with the bird apparently relishing the bitter taste, perhaps because most seeds are bitter. Most parrots eat red peppers with relish. Ornithologists tell us that the birds do have taste buds but that these are situated at the back of the mouth. I am of the opinion that parrots recognize sweetness and like it. I think birds select their food more by sight and instinct than by taste. It is often difficult to change a bird from one seed to another, and sometimes it can be done only by intermingling the new seed with the old and gradually eliminating the old. Parrots seem to like salt; at least this is the only way I can account for the way some parrots love to lick their owner's skin.

Not too much research has been done on the sense of taste in birds, but enough has been done to know that, of all birds, parrots probably have the most sensitive sense of taste.

Tongue
The tongues of all the parrots, large and small, are thick, blunt and remarkably sensitive to touch. Even birds as large as the amazons and African greys can eat the tiny seeds found in sprays of millet.

At one time it was thought that parrots used their tongues when imitating the human voice. We know that this is not true and that the tongue is only a poor help, if any, when it comes to speaking. The sounds are formed in the throat. Until quite recently birds were mutilated by having their tongues split to make them loose because it was thought that this enhanced their ability to talk. Such mutilation is, of course, quite useless, and I am happy to report that this vicious practice has virtually died out. How it started I'll never know, because it accomplishes nothing.

The tongues of the nectar-feeding species are longer, more pliant and invariably have brush-like tips to assist them in taking liquid and soft fruit nourishment. These species do not learn to repeat words as well as do the seed-eating varieties. This has been attributed to their tongue structure, but, considering the minor role the tongue plays in making sounds, I cannot think it is the reason.

Hearing
The parrots, in common with all birds, have their ear apertures concealed by feathers. Because of this, many persons mistakenly believe that birds have no ears. This is far from true. They have a highly acute sense of hearing. If this were not so, how would they learn to mimic

103

sounds so well? It is surprising over what a great distance parrots can hear other birds calling and how quickly they react when hearing their owner's voice.

Vision

The eyes seem to be constructed somewhat on the principle of a telescope, adapting them to long-distance vision. They are situated centrally, and the birds can see backward and forward and up and down as well as (in a limited range) straight ahead.

The intensity of light causes the pupil to dilate or contract. Most parrots move about mainly during the daylight hours, although a few species prefer the dusk. Parrots do not like to move in the dark.

The eyes of some parrots, particularly the larger ones, seem to indicate their feelings. When birds are angry, excited or frightened, their irises will contract almost to pinpoints. This can serve as a warning to owners, who should then take extra care as to how they approach or handle their birds.

Because of the eye placement it is possible for birds to see on both sides at the same time, but they cannot focus both eyes on one object unless it is immediately in front of them. It is generally believed that birds can distinguish different colors and that they can also see the range of shades from black to white. Birds can be frightened by brightly colored fabrics when they are moved suddenly.

Parrots are clever at recognizing human beings; most probably this is because they recognize their clothes. Experiments with changes of clothing suggest that birds recognize the wearing apparel more quickly than they do the face. There are cases on record where birds have not recognized owners who put on eyeglasses.

Generally speaking, parrots have very few eye problems.

Digestion

Food is swallowed whole. It passes down the long esophagus into the crop, which is just beyond the base of the neck, and here it is stored and moistened. When the crop is full it can often be seen protruding at the front of or toward one side of the breast. The crop enables the parrot to eat a large amount of food, save it and digest it later, or regurgitate it to feed its young.

From the crop, food passes by peristaltic (wave-like) movements slowly into the first part of the stomach, known as the proventriculus. Here gastric juice is secreted. The food then passes into a second part of the stomach, the gizzard. This is a tough-walled organ in which the food is ground with grit and pebbles that the bird has also swallowed. As we know, birds have no teeth, so the gizzard acts like a grist mill to crush the food. From the gizzard the food, now in a semi-fluid state, passes into the first part of the small intestine, where the liver and pancreas contribute their necessary secretions and the nutrients are assimilated into the system. The waste matter passes into the large intestine and from there into a chamber, the cloaca, from which it is discharged through the anus, or as it is more commonly called in birds, the vent.

Urine from the kidneys also passes into the cloaca and is excreted along with the solid wastes. Birds do not have a separate external urinary organ nor is the urine of a healthy bird liquid; it is white and semi-solid.

Sex Organs

The body cavity also contains the sex organs, which in the case of the male consist of a pair of testes from which tiny tubes carry sperm to the cloaca. In the act of mating the male bird mounts the female and presses the lips of his cloaca into hers, injecting his sperm.

While the sex of some members of the parrot family can easily be distinguished by the birds' external appearance, chiefly color variations, in most cases it cannot. In fact, with some species even experienced aviculturists cannot be sure. Many times pairs have been sold as "true pairs" only to discover later that both were males or both females. This need not seem so strange when we realize that all of the bird's reproductive organs are *inside* the body cavity. The sex distinctions in those species in which sex can be differentiated visually are discussed in the sections on the individual species.

The female organs consist of an ovary and oviduct. The embryonic female develops two ovaries, but the right one and its duct quickly degenerate, so to all intents and purposes she has only one ovary and one oviduct—the left. Situated near the kidneys at the back of the body cavity, it resembles a tiny bunch of grapes.

Egg-laying

Enclosed in the ovary are thousands of ova or egg cells. These develop while the embryo is still in the egg and they are all there—enough to last the bird's lifetime—when it hatches. These egg cells, with the addition of lecithin (yellow yolk matter) and, later on, albumin (the white) will develop into eggs—fertile or infertile as the case may be. The protein of the albumin and the oils of the yolk are there to nourish the embryo should it develop.

When an ovum is ripe, it breaks away and is drawn into the funnel-like mouth of the oviduct or egg passage. There it may, or may not, encounter the male sperm which, after mating, have "swum" up into the neck of the oviduct. If it does encounter the male sperm, the ovum, of course, is fertilized and will, if all goes well, develop into a bird. It is at this point that the genetic heritage of the bird is established—with male and female each contributing half of the genes.

The egg, fertilized or not, now travels down the oviduct, dividing into two, then four, eight and so on (in geometric progression) cells, and as it travels it collects swirls of albumin secreted by the glands in the oviduct. Finally two enclosing membranes form around the albumin. Shortly before the egg is laid, other glands deposit calcareous matter to form the shell.

Numerous conditions can affect the deposition of calcium on the shell. Among these are nutrition (amount of calcium, phosphorus, manganese and vitamin D ingested by the hen), season, age of the hen, and environmental temperature. For instance, high temperature decreases the amount of calcium deposited on the egg. Hypothermia (low body temperature) causes premature egg expulsion and prevents calcium deposition, resulting in soft-shelled eggs.

Once the shell has hardened, the egg is ready to be laid, its blunt end forward, pointed end back. The walls of the oviduct are equipped with constrictor muscles which exert pressure around the pointed end, pushing it forward, much as wet soap skids out of your hand when you squeeze it. This pressure continues until the egg is laid. Sometimes pressure occurs not only behind the egg but in front of it, and sometimes the egg is soft-shelled, whereupon its yielding surface merely absorbs the constricting pressure. In either case egg-binding will occur and the mother will have to be assisted.

The egg   to be laid passes into the cloaca and out through the vent. It may or may not be fertile. A female parrot may lay eggs even if she has not been impregnated, but an embryo can develop only if she has been. The whole journey varies according to species; in the case of the budgerigar it takes 48 hours.

Development of the embryo can occur only if the eggs are kept warm, and this the parent birds (usually the mother, sometimes the father, sometimes both) do by sitting on them during the variable periods for incubation.

If your pet is accustomed to eating from your hand, sprinkle his medication on a favorite food and coax him to eat.

III Health

When parrots are well-fed and housed under sanitary conditions free from dampness and drafts, they suffer very few ailments. However, certain unforeseen situations may occur and a bird becomes sick. One of the first indications that a bird is off color is its general listlessness, with its feathers fluffed out and possibly its head tucked into its back feathers. Constantly tucking up one foot or closing one or both eyes is also a warning signal. Whenever a bird is in this condition it behooves the owner to examine it carefully to see if the eyes are dull and whether or not the droppings are watery or unusually colored.

The healthy parrot sleeps with his head pulled back into his shoulders. But when he is ill, the head will droop drowsily farther and farther down into his breast. This is an almost certain sign that something is wrong.

The large intestine at its lower end widens into a chamber known as the cloaca. This is the only exit from the body for all the body products—feces, urine, sperm and eggs. Since the urine mixes with the feces, the feces are never hard; however, in a healthy bird neither are they thin and mucous. The bird's digestive system is different from man's; accordingly, it must eat almost constantly. A parakeet can starve to death if it goes without food for 48 hours. This applies to sick birds as well. Never withhold food from a sick bird; on the contrary, tempt it to eat, offering all of its favorite foods. Many ailing birds have died not from what ailed them, but from starvation.

Hand-feeding

As a last resort, if the bird is not eating you must attempt hand-feeding. Boil six ounces of milk and while it is still warm stir in two ounces of maple or pancake syrup. Beat in the yolk of an egg and a pinch of salt. If it is available add 100 milligrams of an antibiotic such as chlortetracycline. This mixture may be refrigerated, with the quantity to be fed warmed to 80°F before use. Feed this with a plastic eyedropper a few drops at a time. Wrap the bird in a towel so he can't struggle and insert the tip of the dropper in the side at the hinge of the upper and lower jaws. Usually even a sick bird will grasp the tip when it is offered to him this way. Allow a drop or two at a time to trickle down his throat. Never squirt, as you may force liquid into his lungs. After every few drops, pause a few minutes for him to swallow. A large parrot can take a dropperful (about 17 drops) every four hours, a smaller bird proportionately less. If diarrhea is present give him a few drops of Kaopectate or milk of bismuth at the same time. Give this separately, not mixed in with the formula.

Most parrots ordinarily drink very little water. Therefore, when medication is to be administered in his water, place a lamp alongside the cage to keep it at 85° to 90°F. This will cause the bird to drink more. This heat, which in itself is beneficial, should be maintained continually for 24 hours a day until the bird is completely cured.

Medication or vitamin supplements in small quantities may also be disguised by sprinkling them on a favorite food such as a banana.

Aspergillosis

This is caused by the inhalation of spores from various molds, the most common being *Aspergillus fumigatus*. The spores can be airborne into the aviary, or they can develop on moldy seed. Just a few spores start the trouble. Sometimes seed stored in a damp room grows moldy in the bag or bin, or seeds dropped by the birds and not immediately eaten get moldy on the floor of the aviary. Moldy bread or crackers can also be a cause. The disease is not contagious; however, several birds can contract it at the same time from the same source.

An ordinary eyedropper can be used for giving not only liquid medication but also soft food to a sick bird. Photo by L. van der Meid.

The spores attack the lungs and air sacs, causing a cheese-like pus to accumulate. As the infection develops, the infected birds have difficulty breathing, lose their desire for food and, consequently, grow steadily weaker. Some sick birds will stretch their necks and shake their heads as though trying to rid themselves of the blockage.

To date, no satisfactory treatment has been discovered. I would suggest, however, that any suspected case be reported to your veterinarian, as a new drug may have since been developed.

It behooves every bird owner to make sure that the seed he feeds is always fresh, clean, free from mold, that no seed is allowed to mold on the floor of the aviary and that there is no chance of spores being blown into the aviary or cage from a nearby accumulation of wet hay or sawdust litter. Obviously if the aviary does become infected, it will have to be cleaned and thoroughly disinfected. The sick birds will have to be destroyed and the aviary or cage sprayed with a 1% copper sulphate solution before it is ever used again.

109

Asthma

As a general rule this respiratory condition rarely affects parrots housed in aviaries, and only occasionally indoor pets. The first symptoms of asthma are a wheezing noise made when breathing and a general listlessness. If treatment is given immediately there is a very good chance that the bird will recover completely. There are several inhalants on the market that should be used as directed. An electric vaporizer will be helpful. If it is considered that the attack has been brought about by an overheated room or aviary, the bird should be moved to fresher and cooler air. The sick bird should be fed its usual food as well as fresh fruit, green food and, of course, fresh water.

Do not confuse asthma with pneumonia. Because pneumonia affects the lungs, the bird often has difficulty in breathing causing him to make a gasping noise, usually on inhalation but sometimes also as he exhales. The droppings are usually green and watery, the feathers puffed, and as a rule he will hold his beak open. In the later stages the wings will droop.

A bird thus affected really requires professional care. If this is not available put a 40-watt bulb next to the cage and cover cage, bulb and all with a light blanket. Be sure that the blanket cannot touch the bulb and cause a fire. This should maintain the temperature at a desirable 85° to 90°F. Check with a thermometer and if necessary use a different size bulb to achieve the desired heat. This temperature must be maintained 24 hours a day until a complete cure is effected. Don't worry about the light keeping him awake. He can tuck his head under his wing if he wants to sleep.

Dissolve 100 milligrams of chlortetracycline in two ounces of water and leave this for him to drink. Normally a parrot does not drink much, but the high temperature will make him thirsty. If he is too weak to drink, give him an eyedropperful four times a day. This solution should be made fresh each day.

Broken Limbs

Occasionally, through some unfortunate occurrence a leg or a wing will be broken. This is more likely to occur with the smaller fast-moving species than with the larger, more placid birds. With broken limbs it is always best to have them set correctly by a veterinarian since the birds require careful handling and splinting. Broken bones usually heal quickly if set, and the birds regain normal use of their legs and wings.

Colds

All parrots are liable to contract colds if they are subjected to un-

Although all parrots are tropical, it is amazing how well they are able to stand the cold. This picture of a tourist inspecting a canary-winged parakeet was taken at the Brussels outdoor bird market in February, 1968.

satisfactory weather conditions and when they are molting or laying. The symptoms are similar to those which appear in man. Colds seem to be brought on by viruses which attack the birds when their general resistance has weakened.

The symptoms are usually sneezing, watering of the eyes, ruffled feathers and an air of general listlessness. A bird in this condition should be isolated immediately, placed in a hospital cage and one of the sulfa drugs administered as directed. If it's just a cold, the patient will quickly recover but he should not be returned to his normal quarters until he has had time to regain perfect health.

Coccidiosis

Although coccidiosis is fairly well known to poultry raisers, it does not often affect the parrots, particularly those in cages or on stands. Those in outdoor aviaries can contract the disease if they come into contact with wild birds or even domestic poultry. It is usually introduced into an aviary by the contaminated droppings of starlings or sparrows falling through the wirework. If this is seen happening, the owner

111

should work quickly to correct the condition before the entire aviary becomes infected. Sick birds quickly lose weight and a bloody diarrhea sets in. Fortunately, these days there are excellent sulfa drugs and antibiotics which can quickly bring coccidiosis under control. If this disease is even suspected, consult a veterinarian who will prescribe the right treatment. Here again I cannot emphasize too strongly the necessity to disinfect thoroughly the housing where the birds contracted the disease.

Coccidia are protozoan parasites. The oocytes or spore forms which are passed out in the droppings are a source of infection. If the bird's cage is not kept clean and food drops onto the bottom, he can reinfect himself, thus increasing the severity of the infection.

Constipation

Constipation is more likely to affect those birds kept caged since they do not get enough exercise and may be fed on too many rich dry foods. If a bird seems to have difficulty when voiding, examine its droppings. If they are found to be large, dry and hard, constipation should be suspected. The bird's diet should be adjusted and a more liberal use of fruits and green food made. The first day or so add a few crystals of Glauber (Epsom) salts to the drinking water to start the necessary bowel action. Poppy seed mixed in with the regular seed mixture is very good for easing constipation.

Once cured there is no reason for a recurrence provided the bird receives a proper proportion of fruits and greens in its daily diet. This is one reason why human foods should not be fed to parrots. Sooner or later they are sure to upset the bird's digestion.

Diarrhea

The voiding of liquid evil smelling or strangely colored droppings is a sign of diarrhea. It may or may not be the symptom of some other ailment. There are any number of things that can bring about this distressing condition—stale or fouled seed or other food, frosted or tainted fruits and green food, and contact with other birds suffering from the condition. If a bird shows even slight signs of diarrhea, isolate it at once and keep it warm. If the vent feathers become fouled they should be gently and carefully cleansed with warm water and a good germicide or, if necessary, cut away with sharp scissors.

The patient should be given a course of one of the sulfa drugs as prescribed by a veterinarian. Fortunately these drugs are very effective and will usually cure a sick bird in short order with no bad after effect. They are usually administered directly to the bird in a diluted form, but some can also be offered in the drinking water, which should first be boiled and then allowed to cool. Since sick birds are usually thirsty they will drink enough of the solution to ease their condition. During treatment the bird should be fed its usual seed mixture, but fruits and green food should be withheld until the condition has completely disappeared.

Egg Binding

Normal non-breeding pet hens rarely suffer from egg binding, but it does occasionally occur with nesting birds when the conditions are not favorable. Should a hen be over-fat or become subjected to drafts or chilling cold at the time the eggs are being laid, the condition known as egg binding occurs. A further cause of this distressing condition is the lack of certain minerals in the system, which causes the eggs to be soft-shelled or even shell-less, making them difficult to expel and in extreme cases causing a rupture of the oviduct. Prevention, of course, should always be a prime object. Breeding hens should be kept in fine condition and have access to all the needed mineral elements long before they are mated.

The symptoms of egg binding are easy to see. An affected hen will usually be found sitting with her feathers all fluffed out, eyes half closed, breathing heavily and her vent will be swollen and red. She should at once be carefully picked up and caged by herself in a room with very high temperature. A little olive oil applied gently with a camel hair brush to the swollen vent will be helpful. A half teaspoonful of glycerine should be mixed in with the drinking water; the bird will usually drink this quite readily.

Usually the additional warmth helps the bird to regain her muscular control and expel the egg within a few hours. If this does not happen, the vent should again be oiled and the bird held over a jug of steaming water. This, however, should only be done if she still cannot pass her egg. The sick bird should be handled as little as possible to avoid causing further complications by bruising. Surgical forceps may be inserted into the cloaca to break the egg if all else fails, and as many pieces as possible should then be carefully picked out.

A hen that is chronically egg-bound should not be bred again.

Enteritis

There seem to be two forms of this deadly condition—one which is highly contagious, one which is not. The first is caused by bacteria which can spread quickly if precautions are not taken at once. The second, the non-contagious form, is usually brought on by the bird's eating poisonous material such as rotten, stale or fermented food. In both cases the treatment is the same and the owner must act quickly. The symptoms are fluffing of feathers, dullness of eyes and loose, slimy, green-tinted droppings which in the advanced stage become blood-stained. The treatment is like that outlined under diarrhea, commencing with the complete disinfecting of everything that has come in contact with the sick bird. Here again I feel that the services of a veterinarian should be obtained to effect a quick and complete cure. Even suspected cases should be dealt with promptly, and if this were always done, far more birds would survive.

Fits

Generally speaking, the larger parrots are slow and deliberate and consequently not very likely to suffer from fits. However, some of the smaller, more excitable kinds, such as budgerigars and lovebirds, may occasionally fall victim to this condition. The beginning of the breeding period is the most likely time for fits, and more particularly with male birds. Usually there is little that can be done since the bird will suddenly flutter to the floor and die before the owner discovers it.

If breeding specimens are kept in clean, healthy surroundings, and are well fed on a balanced diet (and are not allowed to become overly excited), fits are unlikely to occur. Some success has been reported in curing fit-affected birds by mouth-to-mouth resuscitation. Should you see the bird fall, lay him on the palm of your left hand, holding his head between your thumb and forefinger. Rest the thumb and forefinger of

A white-crested cockatoo with its claws being trimmed with an ordinary wire cutter. Photo by Dr. H. R. Axelrod.

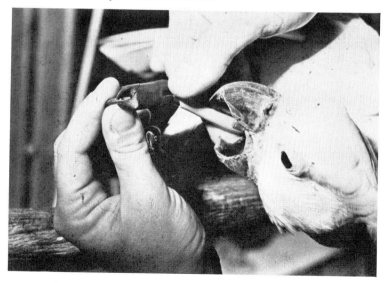

Birds with abnormal plumage, like these budgerigars, regardless of the cause of the condition, should not be utilized for breeding.

your right hand lightly on either side of his chest. Breathe gently directly into his beak and you will see his chest inflate. Now gently press down with your right hand to expel the air and repeat for five to ten minutes or until the bird revives.

French Molt

The feather condition known as French molt can affect any member of the parrot family. Its incidence is so rare that I will just mention the fact that it is thought to be brought about by the inability of the parent birds to pass on certain essential feather-building agents to their young, or when the young themselves are unable to absorb and utilize these agents. The condition is not contagious. There is thought to be a hereditary predisposition, so any affected bird that has been apparently cured should not be used for breeding. The symptoms in the milder cases are loss of some flight and long tail feathers and in the more severe cases these feathers, together with the soft body, wing and neck feathers, molt constantly. The new feathers never complete their full growth but just drop out. This condition has been seen more often in parakeets. Birds so affected always look scraggly and usually cannot fly. They are called runners or creepers. Often the mild cases appear normal again within a few weeks, but, as I have said, they should not be used for breeding as this is possibly an inherited condition.

Impacted Crop

This is not too common a condition in older birds, but it occurs more frequently in young ones. It is the result of swallowing food, usually fibrous food or foreign matter such as string, that sticks in the crop and clogs it. In severe cases pressure on the trachea can suffocate the bird. If this condition exists, the enlarged crop will be obvious. Wrap the bird in a towel and inject a little mineral oil into the crop and try to gently massage the impacted matter out through the mouth. Stringy material can sometimes be hooked out with a button hook. In severe cases, an immediate (but minor) operation by a veterinarian will be necessary.

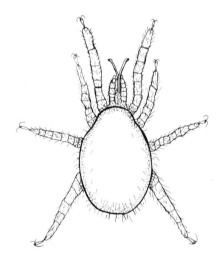

Mites, in contrast to lice which have three pairs of legs, have four pairs. Those mites found in birds are generally very small and are difficult to recognize, except when they are engorged with blood.

Mites and Lice

Birds can be attacked by red mites or feather lice under unsanitary conditions, but fortunately there are ways of combating them.

Red mites are tiny gray insects that do not live on birds but in tiny crevices of the perches, cages, aviaries and often in nesting boxes. They usually come out at night and feast on the blood of the birds and then return to their holes in the morning. They often look red because of the blood they've engorged. If you suspect their presence, throw a piece of white cloth over the cage and check it next morning for tiny red specks.

Feather lice actually live among the feathers of the birds where they eat the flaked skin and feather oil, and stick their eggs to the shafts of the feathers.

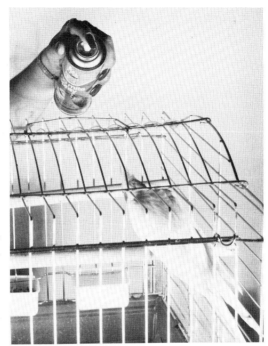

A skin mite attacks the bare areas at the base of the beak and around the eyes, causing the skin to appear rough and crumbly. Smear these areas lightly once a day with mineral oil, but avoid the nostrils. This will drown the parasites and the skin will regrow.

There are a number of commercial products available in pet shops to exterminate these pests. Ask your dealer to recommend one, and follow the directions on the package. The attack must always be made on two fronts—the bird itself and the cage or aviary.

There are on the market insecticides (pest strips) which are incorporated into resin bars. They can be hung close to the cage or in the aviary out of the reach of the birds. They exude a vapor (with little or no odor) which is death to mites and lice as well as flying insects (fruit flies, for instance) which come within the area of effectiveness.

Overgrown Claws and Beaks

It is usually the middle sized and smaller species of parrots that need their claws or beaks trimmed occasionally. Most of the larger ones seem to have the knack of keeping theirs at a useful length. Claws can be cut with small wire cutters, taking care not to cut too high up and sever the blood vessel which feeds the claw. A similar tool can be used for the

117

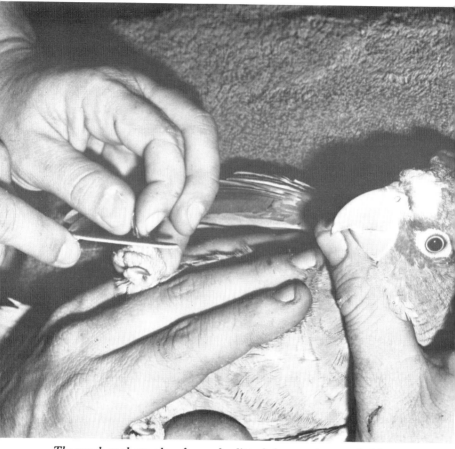

The rough or sharp edge of a newly clipped claw can be smoothed by an ordinary nail file. Photo by Dr. H. R. Axelrod.

trimming of beaks. For smaller birds, nail clippers work well. Here again care must be taken not to cut away too much beak or to cut in too deeply. Frequently just the overgrown tip needs to be snipped off.

If you are not experienced at claw and beak cutting, hold the bird against a strong light. The dark area of the blood vessel can be easily seen in light-colored claws and beaks. It is easier to see if you examine the inner part of the bill as the bird opens it. They always do so to emit a vocal protest at being held. Dark-colored claws and beaks must be cut very slowly, a little at a time. Stop as soon as the cut surface changes texture or signs of blood appear.

Overheating

Never leave a parrot in the hot sun. Indoors or out, the bird should always be able to move from pleasant sunshine into cool shade. These birds are quite susceptible to overheating. Their feathers should always be tightly molded to the body. When they fluff them out, open their wings and "pant" with open beaks, and when pulsing is noted in the upper throat, be warned: the bird is on the verge of sunstroke. Move him quickly into cool shade, but not too quickly; not, for instance, into an air-conditioned room. Fresh cool drinking water will help to reduce the bird's temperature.

Pneumonia

See the discussion under asthma. The early symptoms are much the same.

Psittacosis

The correct name for this ailment is ornithosis, and at one time it was quite erroneously believed to be common among newly imported parrots. Because of this, many countries banned the importation of such birds except under specific safequards. It is caused by a large virus called a rickettsia. These days, with the advent of more hygienic methods of shipping birds and antibiotic drugs, psittacosis is almost a thing of the past.

Choosing a bird immediately after importation gives the advantage of a large group to select from; on the other hand, illness resulting from stress and overcrowding may take a few more days to show up.

The symptoms are a general fluffed out appearance of all feathers and a mucous discharge from mouth and nostrils, accompanied by acute diarrhea. Obviously if psittacosis is suspected the assistance of a veterinarian should be enlisted immediately. As with enteritis, all precautions should be taken immediately.

Regurgitation

When pet birds regurgitate their food it often causes their owners undue alarm because only on rare occasions is there a serious cause. It usually happens when the birds are in fine condition and ready to breed. When another bird is not present they will attempt to feed mirrors, food vessels, toys or even their owner. This can, of course, be unpleasant and necessitate frequent cleaning of the cage. However, it is usually only a phase which soon passes and the birds return to normal. If, on the other hand, regurgitation is caused by bad food, acute indigestion or a cold, it will usually be accompanied by other symptoms that will suggest the underlying cause.

Tumorous Growths

Growths of a fatty nature that appear on the wing and chest areas are fairly simple to remove, but when they appear on the softer underparts treatment becomes more difficult. In cases where surgery may be needed, call on a veterinarian for advice. Most of these soft growths can be cured. However, if the growth is internal, I am afraid there is no known cure at present either by surgery or medication. Sometimes a blocked oil gland situated just at the base of the tail can be mistaken for a tumor. In this case the swollen gland should be gently bathed with warm water and disinfectant and the clogged oil removed with the aid of a cotton-tipped swab.

Wounds

It is possible for parrots to inflict nasty wounds upon one another if a serious quarrel takes place. Should this happen, the combatants must be separated and the wounds washed carefully with warm water and antiseptic, and if the wounds are not too severe they should be dusted with an antiseptic powder. Bad wounds may need suturing by a veterinarian.

Personal Sanitation

An extremely important thing to remember when dealing with any sick bird is the washing of one's hands before and after handling the patient. I find that this practice is not always observed and that diseases are frequently transferred from one bird to another because of the oversight. If gloves are worn these too should be disinfected.

A group of quaker parakeets in a quarantine station awaiting transportation to the United States. The practice of clinging to the wires as close to the top as possible is characteristic of birds. When they are alarmed they always seek safety in height.

IV Collecting Wild Parrots

It may never occur to those of us whose first glimpse of a parrot is in a cage to ask by what route this wild bird arrived. Yet most parrots are sold in the temperate zones, although almost without exception they are creatures of the tropics. Many of them inhabit dense jungles miles from civilization, while others are found in mountain ranges in sparsely inhabited areas. Most parrots travel in flocks ranging from a dozen or so to several thousand individuals.

From South America, Africa and Asia the birds come to us through the hands of native trappers and livestock dealers. Most of them are babies. These young birds may be taken from their nesting holes by native trappers and reared by hand. These birds soon become accustomed to human beings and become very tame, depending wholly on their keepers for food. This consists mostly of boiled corn. At first this has to be forced upon the birds, but later they accept it readily—so readily that it is often difficult to get them off boiled corn and onto the usual dry seed mixtures.

The rather messy condition of the feathers of some newly imported birds is usually the result of their being fed on soft boiled corn and very ripe fruit. Fortunately, when they get their adult feathers after their first molt their plumage becomes perfect.

It can be quite a hazardous task to catch the young birds, as the nest holes may be high up in tall trees, often on dead branches. If the nest is visited when the parents are not away searching for food, the parents may attack the intruder. Serious damage can be inflicted by the powerful beaks of some of the larger species. However, the trappers are well-versed in the habits of the birds they seek, so they are seldom in danger.

Nets are often used to trap adult birds at their watering places and known feeding grounds. Sometimes they are driven into nets fixed at strategic places or nets are dropped on them from above as they feed or drink. These adults have to be handled with extreme skill to avoid injury.

Some species cannot be caught by nets because of their particular methods of feeding. In such cases the trappers resort to treating branches of trees with a strong adhesive. This is effective only for the smaller species; the larger birds are just too strong. Except for an occasional missing claw, birds captured this way suffer no harm.

When adult birds are caught the trappers usually clip the flight feathers on one wing to prevent the birds from flying. This is why many newly imported birds have full flights on only one wing. This cutting does not hurt the birds in any way, and the feathers are replaced by new ones when the birds molt.

In the native villages a great deal of the feeding is done by children and women. The birds are housed in all manner of crude cages made of tough wood bound together with vines. Some birds are tethered with strips of leather to wooden perches under a thatch of grass. It is a most interesting sight to see native children feeding a wide variety of birds, many of them as tame and friendly as puppies.

When the trappers have made a sufficient haul they transport the stock to a local market or to an export dealer. The method of transportation varies: it may be by river boat, on the backs of pack animals or on poles slung between two bearers. Having delivered their birds and received payment, the trappers return home with instructions for the next consignment.

One parrot dealer who lives most of the year in the South and Central American jungles has given me this first-hand account of a parrot collecting expedition which he accompanied.

The village from which the expedition was to start was a small collection of native huts. For the most part they were built of adobe with thatched roofs. The more affluent had wooden structures. The houses were laid out in a haphazard fashion, although in general they followed the pattern of a wide central street ending in a plaza or market square. The streets were beaten earth which was turned into a quagmire during the rainy season. There was no sewerage. Sanitation was aided by packs of dogs which roamed the village looking like animated skeletons stitched together with flesh, (to avoid confusion) and by buzzards. In spite of what to us would seem obvious discomforts, the people all seemed quite content.

The parrot collectors all gathered at 3 a.m. It is cold in the jungle at that time and a heavy mist soaks everything, but a cup of steaming hot coffee without sugar seemed to put new vigor into my limbs and in a short time we were ready to start. The area in Mexico where the collecting was to be done was a flat open plain with a peculiar sort of clay-like surface which resembled Fuller's earth. Nothing grew there at that time. The nets were stretched loosely between poles about ten feet high with three sets being joined together to make one thirty-foot fencelike affair. By five o'clock all the nets were set up, a few tame birds were left in the middle and we all hid. I was told you could set your watch by the arrival of the scouts. Precisely at 6 a.m. the advance guard of the flock, which was eventually to number several thousand, arrived to survey the area. These were followed by ever-increasing numbers of parrots coming from the jungle or mountains nearby. The volume of their shrieks was deafening as they settled down and began waddling about busily picking up the clay-like material. Apparently, there was something in it which satisfied a need or a desire because they pecked the material avidly.

Now, while a parrot settles to the ground almost vertically (like a helicopter), when it takes off it must fly almost horizontally (like an airplane) until it has gained height; and

One method of capturing parrots is to mark the location of their roosts as they stream toward them in great numbers at twilight. This is a rose-breasted cockatoo returning to his resting place for the night. Photo by H. Müller.

so, when these birds attempted to leave the "feeding" ground they began colliding with the nets. The force of their flight caused a little bag to form which neatly held the parrot in place until he could be removed and put with others into wicker baskets for transportation. About ten birds (mostly redheads) were all that the net could hold before the weight of their bodies stretched it so taut that newcomers were not empouched.

I was told that in this one local area a trapper could catch 100 to 150 birds a day, day after day, without depleting the population. I was also told that during the rainy season, which lasts for three months, all the birds disappear and no one knows where they go. Many efforts have been made to locate their rainy weather habitat, but so far these efforts have been fruitless. At that time of the year the clay plains themselves are under water so the parrots stay away.

This clay, of course, is not their diet; it seems to be some sort of supplement which may act as a source of minerals. Later in the day they leave for their feeding grounds. In cultivated areas they do a great deal of damage to the farmer's crops. They are particularly fond of sweet corn and will strip a field if given opportunity. In Peru, they also use nets to trap golden-winged conures and other small parrots. However, because these birds are lighter and more agile, a different method is used. The trappers have tamed parrots which are used as callers. Again, the traps are set up before dawn in the form of a rectangle with the callers, or Judas birds, in the center. These birds are completely tame—they are not pinioned, their wings are not clipped, nor are they drugged or fastened in any way. They know their job and seem to enjoy it. As dawn appears, the callers begin chattering. Their calls are soon answered by wild birds, and gradually the flocks begin to gather. When enough have settled among the nets, a trigger is released and the nets fall, their weight holding the birds down. This way, the conures are never hurt and great numbers can be trapped at one time.

Still another method of capturing birds, I was told, is to mark the location of their roosts as the parrots stream toward them in great numbers at twilight. When the jungle night has settled, the trapper, who must be extremely agile, climbs the trees and captures each bird by hand. He carries a bag into which each startled bird is popped so as to leave his hands free for more. This also requires great dexterity as wild parrots have powerful bills and naturally resent being snatched up suddenly. This can be done only in the dark of the moon, because if there is any light at all the birds will become alarmed and fly away. While it is true that they only blunder about in the dark, nevertheless this would place them beyond the reach of the trapper.

Macaws are also caught by noticing the trees which they use for roosts. Unfortunately for them, most birds tend to return to the same area and even to the same limb night after night. The trappers mark these trees and while the birds are away place rope snares consisting of hundreds of little loops over the branches. If even one claw is caught by a loop, it is enough to hold the bird until the trapper can climb the tree and capture it.

The birds are taken to the native villages to be kept there until Saturday. Saturday was market day in Iquitos, Peru, my informant's headquarters, and on that day all the natives made their way to the city carrying their week's catch to be offered for sale. It is interesting that although bananas are not normally grown in that area, they are imported to be used as bird food. This is all that the birds are fed during their captivity, and they seem to thrive upon it. So far as I could ascertain, no nuts, seeds or any other types of fruits were fed, although in the wild they eat all of these. However, they learn to eat bananas quite readily and seem to enjoy that fruit.

A Congo red-headed parrot (**Poicephalus gulielmi**). *Photo by H. V. Lacey.*

Part III Species of Parrots

I Old World Parrots: Africa and Asia

Blue-crowned Hanging Parakeet *(Loriculus galgulus)*

Habitat: Malay Peninsula, Sumatra

These are members of a small group of tiny parrots, most of them less than six inches long, which have the strange habit of spending most of their lives in upside down positions.

The blue-crowned is green with a blue patch at the top of the head, a yellow patch at the back and a red one in front. There is also a yellow bar at the lower back. The hen birds are duller and lack the red throat patch and yellow band. The designation of parrot or parakeet is interchangeable.

In captivity, they are fed like the lories on soft fruits and nectar, and like lories they are inclined to be messy in their feeding habits. Their claws grow long and require frequent trimming. One characteristic to be aware of is that they breathe heavily, even when they are in good health.

Congo Red-headed Parrot *(Poicephalus gulielmi)*
Also known as Jardine's parrot and red-crowned parrot
Habitat: Equatorial Africa

These are neat compact little birds of some 11 inches in length, mainly dark green, with head and front, wing butts and thighs all of a pleasing scarlet orange. The sexes are alike in plumage. Unfortunately these attractive birds are rarely imported, and not too much is known about their habits.

Brown-necked Parrot *(Poicephalus robustus)*
Habitat: Equatorial Africa

This parrot is about the same size as the African grey, with a rose-red forehead and the neck and back of head brown to silvery gray—hence the name. The feathers under the rump are bright green, and above it are a dark brownish green. Thighs and wing butts are vermilion red. The horn-gray bill is very powerful.

Senegal Parrot *(Poicephalus senegalus)*
Also known as the yellow-bellied Senegal parrot
Habitat: Africa

This popular parrot is quite small, being only some nine inches in length. It is probably, after the grey, the most widely kept of the African parrots. The color is quite pleasing, with dark gray necks and heads and cheek patches which are a shade lighter. The upper part of the chest is green and the lower part a bright yellow orange. The color of these birds varies a little according to the area from which they originate. Some birds show more yellow in their plumage, and it might be possible by controlled breeding to enlarge these yellow areas. Senegal parrots will nest in captivity and, like the African greys, they make excellent parents.

It is generally believed that these parrots are the easiest of all to train to perform all kinds of antics, and they are always gentle with their owners. They make excellent cage birds. Once fully acclimated, Senegals will also live happily in an aviary. They seem to be able to stand quite low temperatures without trouble, provided they are well-housed in dry, draftproof sleeping quarters. There are three subspecies which sometimes turn up in shipments of the common Senegals.

Moustache Parakeet *(Psittacula alexandri)*

Also known as the banded or red-breasted parakeet

Habitat: India and Burma into China

A huge black "moustache" reminiscent of the "Gay 90's" identifies this magnificent bird. It has another line of black over the beak from eye to eye. The overall color is green, but the entire head, cheeks and throat are lilac. The breast is more of a plum color with a blush of violet. The belly has a touch of pale blue. There is a greenish yellow patch on the otherwise green wing; the very long slender tail is blue-green and the beak a fiery red.

Length: Approximately 15 inches.

The female differs in that she has a black beak and is in general duller, with no lilac on the throat and very little blue on the belly.

The moustache parakeet is a hardy bird that does well in western aviaries; it has been wintered out of doors.

Blossom-headed Parakeet *(Psittacula roseata)*

Also known as plum-head

Habitat: India, Pakistan, Burma

"Of all the old world parrots," writes W.T. Greene, "this is, without exception, the most elegantly formed, the most beautiful, docile, and desirable." They are slender, elegant creatures. Their head is red washed with blue, suggesting the bloom on a plum. The black stripes extending from the mandibles form a collar around the neck, the top of the wing is marked by a red spot and the underwing coverts are azure blue. The females lack the black collar, replacing it with a ringlet of pale yellow. Their heads are more lilac than plum color; the tips of their tails are also pale yellow.

Blossom-heads take kindly to aviary life and breed quite readily. As parents, they are generally very attentive and extremely fond of their broods. In the wild, four to six broad oval eggs are laid in a nest hole excavated out of a hollow tree, and a similar nest hole should be provided in the aviary.

Derbyan Parakeet *(Psittacula derbiana)*

Habitat: Tibet, China

These are one of the larger (20 inches overall length) members of the ring-neck family. Their attractive coloring keeps them in demand. Unfortunately, they are not readily obtainable these days because their native home is in southeastern Tibet and southwestern China, areas pretty much closed to the rest of the world. The few specimens seen at

Senegal parrot, **Poicephalus senegalus** *(male). Photo by H. Müller.*

Blue-crowned hanging parakeet, **Loriculus galgulus** *(male). Photo by K. Paysan.*

Ring-necked parakeets are easily trained. Photo by L. van der Meid.

cage bird exhibitions or in private collections are always a center of attraction.

Their main color is bright green, the head and breast soft lilac, with more bluish tint at the forehead. A band of black runs from eyes to beak and to a large moustache which is also black, contrasting strongly with the lilac. The wings have a soft bright yellowish green patch; this color also appears on the thighs and vent. The cock's beak is red, the hen's black.

Alexandrine Parakeet *(Psittacula eupatria)*
Also known as large Indian parakeet; Indian rock parrot; Alexander ring-neck

Habitat: Afghanistan to India, Sri Lanka and Burma

These are the largest of the ring-necked group, being some 21 inches in length including their long narrow tails. When the confidence of an Alexandrine has been gained it will train quite readily and learn to talk a little.

I quote W.T. Greene:

> The Alexandrine Parrot, if named after the great Emperor of Macedonia, deserves the appellation, for he is, literally, the greatest of his race, measuring some 20 inches in extreme length, twelve of which, however, are occupied by the tail; the body is slim and compactly made, but the head is large, and the beak of formidable dimensions; still

his majesty can scarcely be called a handsome bird, nor is he of exactly royal, not to say imperial aspect; but he is not a bad fellow nevertheless, and, if taken young, can be made a very agreeable companion.

The prevailing color of the plumage is grass green, the back of the neck is marked by a broad crescentic patch of pinky rose; and a narrow ring of black, starting from the insertion of the mandibles, on both sides, passes round the neck, forming a complete circle; the beak is orange-red, and there is a large dull red spot on the shoulder on either side.

He goes on to say:

It is somewhat doubtful whether this or the smaller Ring-necked species is the bird that was known to the ancients, the parrot of which Aristotle and Pliny wrote, and in honor of whom Horace composed one of his most charming poems.

It is also called the Indian rock parrot because it has been known to breed in cliffs and in crumbling walls. In India and other parts of their habitat they inhabit niches and crevices in the great stone palace and fortress walls, where visitors may see them flitting about like pigeons do in western cities. The late Duke of Bedford claimed that they are extremely hardy birds, adding that in all his years of keeping Alexandrines he had never seen a sick or dead one.

Slaty-headed Parakeet *(Psittacula himalayana)*
Habitat: Northern India, Himalayas, northwestern China

Care must be taken not to confuse this species with the female blossom-head, which slate-heads greatly resemble in color although they are much more substantial in body, being some 17 inches long.

They make excellent birds for cage or aviary but they are not too common in the bird markets. Owners of slate-heads state that the birds are at first timid and inclined to be wild, but when they settle down and their confidence has been gained they become quite friendly and readily take food from the hand. They learn to repeat a few words and become quite good at whistling.

Their main color is green, with the whole of the head a slate blue which turns black at the base to form a collar which runs from the nape to the lower part of the beak. The cock's beak is red as is his shoulder patch, and the tail feathers are tipped with white. The hen's shoulder patch is absent, and her slate blue head is some shades paler.

Blossom-headed parakeet, **Psittacula roseata** *(male). Photo by A. van den Nieuwenhuizen.*

Opposite, top: A pair of moustache parakeets, **Psittacula alexandri fasciata** *(male with red bill). Opposite, bottom: ring-neck parakeet,* **Psittacula krameri** *(male). Photos by H. Muller.*

133

Ring-neck Parakeet *(Psittacula krameri)*

Also known as the common ring-neck, Bengal parakeet, rose-ringed parakeet, green parakeet

Habitat: India, Africa

"This most delightful of all the longtails," writes the German ornithologist Dr. Karl Russ, "is also that which was first known in Europe; it is mentioned by Aristotle, and described by Pliny. Many specimens of these parrots were brought to Rome from Africa under Nero. It is the only member of the family common to both Asia and Africa."

This species is usually called the common ring-neck to distinguish it from its larger cousin, the Alexandrine. It is physically distinguished by the fact that it lacks the maroon shoulder patches. The ring-neck is some 16 inches overall in length and is mainly bright green. The neck is ornamented by a band of rose red which turns to bluish at the upper edge; the moustache and eye streaks are black and the beak red with a dark tip. The hens and immature birds lack the characteristic ring markings.

Most ring-neck males can be taught to say a few words, and occasionally the females will learn to imitate. They are excellent aviary birds which breed quite readily and have become almost domesticated. Several color forms are bred in captivity; these are the yellow, the lutino (red-eyed yellow) and the blue. These colors are inherited in the normal Mendelian pattern. They make good parents, often rearing two nests a year.

Long-tailed Parakeet *(Psittacula longicauda)*

Habitat: Malay Peninsula

These are truly magnificent birds with a six-inch body and a tapering ten-inch tail. This fine appendage has given them their name, but they are also called Malaccan parakeets because of their native haunt. This species does not take too kindly to cage life, but it is quite happy in large flighted aviaries when given a reasonable amount of cover.

The top of the head is vivid green; cheeks and nape are rosy pink, paler at the back and edged with black to form a ring. The walrus-type moustache is wide and black, tapering to a point near the shoulders. The unusual beak is rose red on top and black below in cock birds; in the hens brown replaces the red. The overall color is soft green, deeper on the upper parts. When it reaches the lower breast and under the tail it becomes heavily suffused with yellow. The tail has two blue central feathers that are about six inches longer than the rest of the tail. Hen birds have a shorter tail and lack the depth of pink on the face and the black markings.

African Grey Parrot *(Psittacus erithacus)*

Habitat: Equatorial Africa

It is the consensus of all who know parrots that the African greys are the most gifted of all the Old World parrots. They are easy to handle, gentle of nature, long lived and have a huge capacity for learning and imitating the human voice and other sounds. With care on the part of their owners they can be taught to say the right thing at apparently the right time, giving the impression that they really know what it's all about!

African greys are medium sized parrots some 13 inches in length, with stout hooked beaks and light colored eyes (in adults, but dark when young) surrounded by areas of bare white skin. The hens are almost always smaller than the cocks. The back, wings and underparts are a soft dove gray set off by tail and under coverts that are spectacularly red.

When first imported, African greys and their near relations need special care until they are fully acclimated, but then, if managed well, they are trouble-free. They do very well on a simple diet but need an added quantity of large canary seed. Although these are quite big birds, it is surprising how adept they are at shelling the small canary seeds and eating millet from the spray. Without a doubt millet is highly beneficial to them and helps to keep them in hardy condition.

African greys are bred in captivity quite regularly, and once a pair has started to breed they usually do so for many years.

Timneh Grey Parrot *(Psittacus erithacus timneh)*

Habitat: Equatorial Africa

This subspecies of the African grey is slightly smaller than its relative and much darker gray in color, with the tail and under coverts chocolate maroon as opposed to the bright red of its cousin. This is not a common subspecies, but the birds that are imported invariably turn out to be gentle and intelligent. They require the same treatment as the African grey.

LOVEBIRDS

This interesting group of small short-tailed parrots is quite distinct from the budgerigars which are sometimes mistakenly called lovebirds. Many people are attracted to them because of their attractive colors and extremely friendly behavior toward their mates. There are some nine or

Brown-necked parrots, **Poicephalus robustus.** *Photo courtesy of Vogelpark Walsrode.*

Ring-neck parakeet, **Psittacula krameri**. *Photo by A. van den Nieuwenhuizen.*

ten species. All originally came from the African continent, but nowadays several species are domesticated and bred in captivity. The name "lovebird" is probably due to the affectionate way in which the birds will nestle together and gently preen each other. Greene thinks their name is inappropriate:

> There is a prevalent opinion abroad that these birds are so affectionately attached to each other, that if one dies, the other is certain not long to survive it; hence the rather inappropriate name of "Love Bird," for alas, for the romantic notion: the inseparable will live very well in single blessedness, and trouble himself, or herself, not one whit about the "dear departed."

Several of the species have produced mutations, and interesting new colors have evolved. These new colors, and the ease with which most of the lovebirds breed, have also contributed to their popularity. There are cases on record where single lovebirds taken as pets have become extremely tame and friendly, even learning to say a few words. Some species are quite rare and are only seen in extensive collections. Others are an everyday sight in aviaries, gardens and bird shops.

In addition to being good breeders they make excellent subjects for exhibition, and many fine examples are displayed at shows all over the world. They are easy to manage and reasonably hardy if given dry and draft-proof quarters during cold weather.

They need a seed mixture like that fed to budgerigars, with the addition of a little hemp, oats and sunflower seeds. They are partial to green food and vegetables but not as partial to fruits.

Lovebirds are nest-builders, which is unusual in the parrot family. During breeding times they should be supplied with small twigs and small branches of non-poisonous wood with the bark still on so it can be stripped and used as nesting material. They will also make do with dried coarse grasses, short lengths of straw and even moss. They nest in damp peat, sawdust, wood chips or decayed wood. Best results seem to be obtained when the nesting boxes are hung in the open so that they receive natural moisture.

Madagascar Lovebird *(Agapornis cana)*
Also known as gray-headed lovebird

Habitat: Southwestern Madagascar

These lovebirds differ in looks from the other members of the family, which is understandable since they come only from the island of Madagascar, a quite exotic habitat. They are chiefly green in color,

Lovebirds characteristically nestle together and preen each other. Photo by Dr. H. R. Axelrod.

lighter on the underparts and darker on the wings, with the cock-birds having dove gray on the head, neck and top of the breast. The hen birds are easily identified by the fact that their heads are green.

It takes the Madagascars some time to settle down in new surroundings, but once accustomed to their new home they become tame and friendly. There are records showing that cock Madagascars have learned to imitate a few words. So far they have proved difficult but not impossible to breed in captivity.

I have heard rumors that Madagascars have been crossed with budgerigars and hybrids reared, but to date they remain merely rumors.

Fischer's Lovebird *(Agapornis fischeri)*

Habitat: Tanzania

These are slightly smaller than the masked lovebirds (five and a half inches), but like them they breed freely in captivity. In fact, they breed almost as readily as shell parakeets. The bill is red and the general plumage various shades of green. The forehead is orange red, less brilliant at the cheeks and throat and gradually merging into gold. The top of the head is brownish gold turning to yellowish on the neck. The cere and bare skin around the eye are white. Here again the hen birds are stouter in build, particularly in the head area.

Next to the masks, they are the most popular breeding species. This is undoubtedly helped by the existence of a yellow variety. The Fischer's is a hardy bird and does well in outside aviaries provided it is given draft-proof sleeping quarters.

African grey parrot, **Psittacus erithacus.** *Photo by T. Caravaglia.*

A group of Fischer's lovebirds, **Agapornis fischeri.** *Photo by Dr. H. R. Axelrod.*

Peach-faced lovebird, **Agapornis roseicollis.** *Photo by P. Kwast.*

Nyasa Lovebird *(Agapornis lilianae)*

Also known as Lilian's lovebird

Habitat: Tanzania, Zambia, Malawi and Mozambique.

The Nyasa is only about five inches long. Its general color is green, light on the underparts, dark on the back and wings, turning a yellow-green on the rump and upper tail coverts. The head is "tomato red," brighter on the forehead and crown, paler on cheeks, throat and upper breast. The back of the head is washed with gold. The tail's two central feathers are green. The eye is brown, the beak red. The cere and ring around the eye are bare white skin. The sexes are much alike although the female's head coloring is less bright.

Nyasas are considered the most friendly of all lovebirds. To date, however, their breeding in the U.S.A. has not been too successful.

Lovebirds are bred in large numbers by commercial breeders and by some individuals. Note the millet spray needed to keep them in breeding condition. Photo by G. S. Axelrod.

A masked lovebird (Agapornis personata). Photo by L. van der Meid.

Masked Lovebird *(Agapornis personata)*

Habitat: Tanzania

These are probably the most popular lovebirds because they are such good-natured little birds. Their overall length is just under six inches, with the hen bird usually a little stouter in the head and with a larger upper beak than her partner's. However, this cannot be taken as a positive way of differentiating the sexes since there is such a variety of types in captivity. The bill is red and the eye ring white. The head is blackish brown, more golden tinted at the lower neck and upper back, with the breast clear yellow and richer in color at the throat. The lower body, wings and back are green, and the rump is gray-blue. The tail, as with all lovebirds, is short, square and green in color.

Several mutations have occurred. The most commonly seen is the blue mask. Here the markings are the same as the normal bird's, but all yellow has been replaced by white and all green by blue. There also exists a white variety and a lutino.

A pair of masked lovebirds, blue mutation, **Agapornis personata.**

Opposite, top: A trio of Abyssinian lovebirds, **Agapornis taranta** *(male with red on head). Photo by H. Müller. Opposite, bottom: A pair of masked lovebirds,* **Agapornis personata** *(female in foreground). Photo by A. van den Nieuwenhuizen.*

Generally speaking, lovebirds are best bred in single pairs with the exception of the black-cheeked, Fischer's and Nyasa, which are not so quarrelsome during the breeding period. It may seem strange to talk about these birds fighting, as this seems to contradict their names, but their love is reserved primarily for their mates.

Peach-faced Lovebird *(Agapornis roseicollis)*

Also known as rosy-faced lovebirds

Habitat: Southern Angola

This is one of the larger of the lovebirds, being about six inches long. The general color of the plumage is grass green, the forehead scarlet, the cheeks and throat rosy red. The rump and upper tail coverts are sky blue, the under surface of the wings is blackish gray, the beak is greenish gray and the tail is green with reddish, blue and black diagonal bands. There are records, however, of color mutations. The female's face is fainter than the male's. This is the only difference between the sexes.

The peach-faced has the reputation of being "spiteful" with smaller birds. They usually do better in aviaries than in cages. They are easily bred. In spite of its disposition, the peach-faced is highly popular in the U.S.A. They sometimes carry their nesting material tucked in the feathers of their tail.

Abyssinian Lovebird *(Agapornis taranta)*

Also known as black-winged lovebird

Habitat: Eritrea, Ethiopia

These are the largest of the group, and very handsome birds they are too, but unfortunately they are not free-breeders; while they have been bred from time to time in captivity, they cannot be classed as a sure-breeding variety. Abyssinian lovebirds kept as single household pets have often responded very well indeed. I have no record of any of them learning to mimic, but I think it might be possible with patience.

The bill is dark red. In the male the forehead and eye ring are a different and brighter shade of red, the female lacks the red of the head and eye area. The upper parts of the body are green, with the rump, tail coverts and underparts a lighter shade of green. The wing coverts and primaries are blackish brown, and the tail feathers are green with a wide black band near the tips. The length is between six and seven inches.

Experience has shown that Abyssians can be kept in an aviary with some of the larger parakeets, with which they seem to get on very well. This of course is an advantage since it will add variety to a collection.

A blue-fronted amazon parrot **(Amazona festiva).** *Photo by H. V. Lacey.*

II New World Parrots: North, Central and South America
AMAZON PARROTS

The amazon parrots are the most widely kept of all. This is readily understandable when we realize that there are about 60 different species and subspecies. Accurate identification of specimens is often difficult because of overlapping ranges, local color variations, the probability of interbreeding between various species and also the fact that the plumage color changes with age. Not all of the species are freely imported, but an occasional unique specimen will come into the hands of the importer in a mixed consignment. Since amazons make up such a large group, they vary considerably in size (from 8 to 21 inches), although they all do have one thing in common—the predominance of green in their plumage.

The vast majority of amazons take exceedingly well to captivity both as household pets and as free-flying aviary birds. Those housed in aviaries have been known to nest.

There are some who claim that their power of mimicry is not as great as the African greys, but there are also many who will dispute this. No one can deny that they can develop quite considerable vocabularies. Ability varies with individual birds and, of course, with individual trainers. It is difficult to decide just which variety is the most popular; it seems evenly divided among the blue-fronted, yellow-fronted and the Levaillant's or double yellow-head. Probably the popularity of a particular species at any given time is largely determined by availability and price.

Yellow-lored amazon, **Amazona xantholora**. *Photo by W. de Grahl.*

Opposite: Madagascar lovebird,
Agapornis cana. *Photo courtesy*
of San Diego Zoo.

All amazons are New World birds. They come from Mexico, Central and South America and the islands of the West Indies.

As we mentioned, amazon parrots are for the most part predominantly green, the major color distinction being the different head patterns.

Blue-fronted Amazon *(Amazona aestiva)*
Also known as the turquoise-fronted parrot

Habitat: Brazil, Argentina, Paraguay

These are about average size for amazons, being some 14 inches in overall length and stoutly built. The basic color is green with varying shades of blue on their foreheads, merging into yellow at the top of the head, cheeks, throat and upper breast. The wings are edged with red. There is only a small amount of blue on the juvenile's head, the area increasing with age. There are slight variations in the exact areas of these colors according to the age of the bird and its original habitat.

Most owners agree that blue-fronts are easy to train and quick to learn both words and sounds. This, of course, makes them attractive pets. In fact, they are considered among the top five parrots when it comes to talking ability. Their hardiness and freedom from many of the troubles that affect parrots make them much sought after, as does their life span, which is considerable.

The female is somewhat smaller, particularly around the head and beak, but her plumage is much the same as the male's.

They thrive well on the average parrot seed mixture and seem particularly fond of fruit. This, however, should be given only in moderation. As with all parrots, it is important that they not be fed from the family table, particularly meats, fats and sweets.

Active Amazon *(Amazona agilis)*
Also known as all-green amazon

Habitat: Jamaica

These small parrots (10½ inches) make very good pets although their vocabulary is limited. They handle well and become extremely friendly. Their overall color is green with the feathers edged in a darker shade. The top of the head is bluish tinted, and the primary coverts are red.

Spectacled Amazon *(Amazona albifrons)*
Also known as red, white and blue parrot and white-browed amazon

Habitat: Mexico

The small amazon, less than a foot long, makes a nice friendly pet and, although at times these birds are inclined to screech a little, they do learn to talk reasonably well. They are also particularly easy to tame. They are attractive because of their coloring, the front part of the head being red extending around the eyes, with the forehead and crown white and bright blue. Red and blue also appear on the wings, while most of the green feathers on the neck have black edges. Spectacled amazons are hardy birds that make interesting and colorful aviary specimens as well as family pets.

Orange-winged Amazon *(Amazona amazonica)*

Habitat: Colombia, the Guianas, Venezuela and the islands of Trinidad and Tobago

It is green with yellow crown and cheeks and a blue forehead and lores. In the adults, the yellow on the crown forms a circle. The wing secondaries are orange, and there is orange on the inner web of the tail feathers crossed by a green band. The tail when spread shows a pale scarlet base.

Red-lored Amazon (Amazona autumnalis)

Also known as the yellow- or orange-cheeked amazon.

Habitat: Southern Mexico and Central America

The red-lored amazon is a large bird that varies greatly in size and weight. It averages from 12 to 13 inches long and can weigh anywhere from ten ounces to a pound.

As with all Amazons, its basic color is dark green with the lower parts yellow green. The forehead and lores are bright red. The feathers of the crown and back of neck are edged with lavender. The flight feathers have deep blue tips, with a red patch on the secondaries. The cheeks are chrome yellow or reddish orange. But none of this colorful pattern is clean cut, and the colors are softly blended. The feet are gray, and the eyes are surrounded by yellow-white bare skin.

Individuals of the species vary greatly. Some are noisy, some develop intense likes and dislikes, but most of them make talented and tractable pets.

Mealy Amazon *(Amazona farinosa)*

Also known as the blue-crowned parrot

Habitat: Guianas, Ecuador, Peru and Brazil

The mealy amazon, one of the largest and most impressive-looking members of the amazon group, averages about 16 inches in length. It gets its name from the fact that its head and shoulders have a "powdery" or "mealy" look. Its green plumage has a dull gray tone, darker above than below. The crown and back of the neck have a bluish lilac tint, and there is a patch of yellow or orange red on the crown. Conspicuous is a red wing patch. The tail is green at the base; the beak a light horn color.

Festive amazon, **Amazona
festiva**. *Photo by T.
Caravaglia.*

Blue-fronted amazon, **Amazona aestiva**. *Photo by A. van den
Nieuwenhuizen.*

Red-lored amazon parrot,
Amazona autumnalis.
Photo by T. Caravaglia.

Five amazon parrots. From left to right: Red-lored amazon parrot,
Amazona autumnalis; two orange-winged amazons, *Amazona amazonica;* blue-fronted amazon, *Amazona aestiva;* and mealy amazon, *Amazona farinosa.* Photo by T. Caravaglia.

Amazons enjoys healthful wing-flapping exercises. Photo by L. van der Meid.

Its behavior and treatment are much like the blue-fronted amazon. The mealy, once acclimated, is a very hardy bird and can even be wintered in an outdoor aviary.

Blue-crowned Amazon *(Amazona farinosa guatemalae)*
Also known as the Guatemalan amazon
Habitat: Guatemala, Honduras, southern Mexico
This is a large bird about 16 inches in length and heavily built. It has a striking and commanding appearance and makes a most attractive pet that can develop an extensive vocabulary. Individual birds may be a little shy at first, but taken collectively they are most affectionate and trainable. Blue-crowns are inclined to attach themselves to one member of a household and will then let that person do almost anything with them, but when it comes to strangers caution is necessary.

The large head is blue, brighter at crown and forehead, shading into a powder blue at nape and mantle. The large eyes have clear-cut naked white rings and are deep orange in color. The overall coloring is dark green shading to blue in places. Their beaks are dark but not black and there is some blue and red on the long wing feathers. The blue-crown should not be confused with the mealy, which it closely resembles. Although related, the mealy is a more somberly clad species lacking the large blue area on the head.

Festive Amazon *(Amazona festiva)*

Habitat: Amazon Valley, eastern Peru and Ecuador

These birds are medium sized, about 14 inches to 16 inches in length, and mainly green in color. Their bright spot is the rump, which is a delightful brilliant red but unfortunately it is not seen too often as it is usually hidden by the wings. A thin plum red band crosses between the eyes and forehead, and there is a bluish wash on the crown above the eyes, cheeks and throat.

Festive amazons seem to have found more favor in some of the European countries than in the United States. I have talked to a number of owners, and they all speak highly of its talents as a pet and, in a few cases, as an aviary bird. Their lack of color is made up for by their talking ability. They become very tame and friendly with their owner and family. It can be said with perfect confidence that festives make excellent pets.

Finsch's Amazon *(Amazona finschi)*

Also known as lilac-crowned amazon

Habitat: Western Mexico

These are slightly smaller than the green-cheeked amazons, being some 12 inches in overall length. They have a much more squat appearance owing to their broader chests and wing carriage. Their coloring is not so vivid as some of the other amazons, but the arrangement of their soft shades is most appealing. The chest and underparts are green edged with a darker green, give a boldly scalloped pattern. The front of the head is rich plum in color, becoming paler toward the crown and then fading to a soft lavender. The cheeks are light green with the rest of the body green, darker on the upper parts.

They are hard to sex, but, in general, the heads of the cock birds are not quite so flat on the top as in the hens. It is said that hens make even better pets than the males since they are so easy to handle and very gentle. This means that most specimens can be allowed at liberty quite freely to give their owners even more pleasure watching their quaint antics.

Yellow-fronted amazon, *Amazona ochrocephala ochrocephala,* in the process of being "stick trained." Photo by T. Caravaglia.

Yellow-naped amazon, *Amazona ochrocephala auropalliata,* on a typical "parrot stand." Photo by L. van der Meid.

Mexican double yellow-head, *Amazona ochrocephala oratrix.* Photo by T. Caravaglia.

A pair of Wagler's conures, **Aratinga wagleri** (female) in profile. Photo by L. van der Meid.

Weddel's conure, **Aratinga weddellii**.

Panama amazon, **Amazona ochrocephala panamensis**. Photo by L. van der Meid.

Mexican red-head, **Amazona viridigenalis**. Photo by T. Caravaglia.

Amazon parrots generally make good family pets. Photo by Dr. H. R. Axelrod.

A few pairs have been kept in aviaries for attempted breeding, but as far as I know success did not extend beyond egg-laying. The fault may be that the birds were too friendly with their owners and did not apply themselves fully to their natural duties.

Guilding's Amazon *(Amazona guildingii)*
Also called St. Vincent amazon

Habitat: Lesser Antilles

Here we have another large species some 17 inches in overall length and built in proportion. The crown of the head and around the eyes are colored white, with the back of the head and neck a greenish color. The breast, back and wing coverts are a very nice tawny golden brown shade darkening toward the feather edges. The beauty of the wings is seen only when they are extended to show the orange, blue and green. Like the imperial amazon, these birds are rarely seen except in specialized collections.

Imperial Amazon *(Amazona imperialis)*
Habitat: Lesser Antilles

These magnificent specimens are probably the largest of the whole group, being 19 inches in overall length. The head is purple, with the neck feathers a paler purple with darker tips. The breast is wine color, and the flights are bluish black with the secondaries purple and vivid red, set off by the reddish chocolate shade of the tail. All these colors stand out well against the overall green.

It is readily understandable why this variety is called the imperial. It is, unfortunately, rarely found in captivity, and not much is known about its ability to talk.

Cuban Amazon *(Amazona leucocephala)*

Also known as the white-fronted amazon

Habitat: Cuba and Isle of Pines

These are delightful birds only about 12 inches in overall length, but they carry a fine range of bright colors and make a welcome addition to any aviary collection as well as becoming fine household pets.

Their most outstanding color feature is the white on their foreheads, followed by a beautiful soft pink shade on throat and cheeks that spreads down to the chest. At the back of the head is an area of dull slate blue; the neck, chest and underparts are green with heavy dark borders to the feathers. The flanks are strongly suffused with rich maroon forming a "V" at the vent.

Experience has shown that although Cuban amazons are not especially gifted as talkers, they do learn a few words and can become beautifully tame and friendly. I have no record of their being bred in captivity. I feel sure this is because of the difficulty of obtaining a true pair. I see no reason why under normal aviary conditions they should not reproduce. The Duke of Bedford reported that a Cuban and a blue-fronted amazon have been crossed. Considering the difference in size, this is quite surprising.

A Cuban amazon parrot **(Amazona leucocephala).** *Photo by L. van der Meid.*

Golden-crowned conure, *Aratinga aurea*. Photo by T. Caravaglia.

Half-moon conure, *Aratinga canicularis eburnirostrum*. Photo by T. Caravaglia.

Queen of Bavaria conure, *Aratinga guarouba*.

Jandaya conure, *Aratinga jandaya*. Photo by H. V. Lacey.

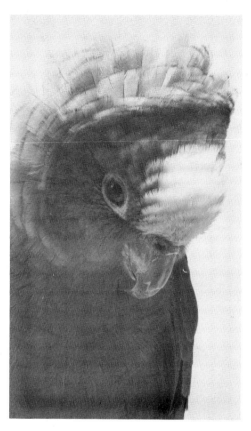

*A yellow-fronted amazon parrot (**Amazona ochrocephala ochrocephala**) showing the characteristic yellow feathers of the crown and front. Photo by H. V. Lacey.*

Yellow-fronted Amazon *(Amazona ochrocephala ochrocephala)*
Also known as the single yellow-head and Colombian amazon
Habitat: Brazil, Ecuador, Venezuela, Trinidad, Peru

These parrots are usually called the single yellow-head, but the name is not very descriptive. They are dark on their upper parts with some dark or black margins to the feathers. The forehead is striped with a pale blue green, and the crown and chin are yellow. In some cases the yellow may extend considerably over the head. The wings are green with red and yellow on the shoulders and blue on the flights—quite a nice combination. They are popular birds and many make good pets. In fact, some owners prefer them to all others, but then every owner of a parrot thinks his pet is the best! Yellow-fronts are hardy birds and, although not many are kept in aviaries, they certainly enjoy themselves when allowed ample flying room. I have known several who liked dogs, particularly big dogs. Like most amazons, they make good talkers.

Yellow-naped Amazon *(Amazona ochrocephala auropalliata)*
Also known as the golden-naped amazon

Habitat: Western Mexico and Central America

Sometimes mistakenly called the Panama amazon, the plumage of this bird is the usual basic green, paler on the breast, but their outstanding feature, as the name implies, is the deep golden yellow on their necks. There is also a small V-shaped area of yellow on the forehead. The flights are blackish blue, and there is a pinkish red bar on the secondaries and a patch of fiery red near the base of the outer tail feathers. They are about 14 inches long. The female's plumage is not so bright as the male's, nor does it have as much sheen. Her beak is narrower, more highly arched, but with a shorter hook.

They learn to talk and, in general, are not noisy birds. Some become extremely affectionate toward their owners, as the species is inclined to attach itself very strongly to one person.

Mexican Double Yellow-head *(Amazona ochrocephala oratrix)*
Also known as Levaillant's amazon and double-fronted amazon

Habitat: Mexico, Yucatan, Honduras

These are extremely popular in the USA as most of them come from adjoining Mexico. Large, stoutly built birds when fully matured, juveniles are much slimmer. The adult birds have large areas of yellow on head and neck which give them their popular name. The area of yellow on the head is limited in young and juvenile birds. Starting with the brow, the yellow area increases with each successive molt until a bird about ten years old is completely and magnificently yellow from the base of his beak, over the head, neck and throat and extending into the shoulders. People familiar with this subspecies can determine their bird's age by the size of the yellow areas. The main color is bright green with red on shoulders, wings and near the base of the tail. There is also some blue on parts of the wings. All told they are an attractive mixture of bright colors. Since young birds are easy to obtain, the possibility of their learning to talk is greatly enhanced. In fact, this variety rivals the African grey for its talking ability.

The female is usually smaller, with a shorter and broader beak. This is difficult to determine when you only have one bird, but select the smallest in a group if you are looking for a female.

Until double yellows have become thoroughly accustomed to a new household, they should be treated with respect since their temper is a little uncertain. Once their confidence has been gained, they make lovable pets.

162

Yellow-naped amazon (left) and Mexican double yellow-head (right). Photo by L. van der Meid.

Panama Amazon *(Amazona ochrocephala panamensis)*

Habitat: Colombia and Panama

This parrot, a much rarer subspecies of *ochrocephala*, is often confused with the double yellow-head and the yellow-naped amazons. Panamas are dark green, but the green on the crown, cheeks, throat and breast has a bluish cast. There is a patch of red on the shoulder and a patch of yellow on the crown. The beak is horn yellow with a darker tip. There is a bare eye ring. The length is 12 to 14 inches.

They learn to talk very well.

Yellow-lored Amazon *(Amazona xantholora)*

Habitat: Yucatan, Belize

These are quite small for amazons, being only about ten inches long. Their main color is green with white on the crown of the head merging into bright blue at the rear. The lores (the space between the eyes and bill) and chin are yellow, with the area around the eyes red and ear coverts very dark.

Mexican Red-head *(Amazona viridigenalis)*

Also known as red-crowned green-cheeked amazon

Habitat: Northeastern Mexico

This is one of the few amazons with a red crown. By nature they are less phlegmatic than are most other amazons; consequently they can be

*A Mexican red-head amazon parrot (**Amazona viridigenalis**). The cheeks of this species are bright green. Photo by C. Bickford.*

vocally demanding at times. As pets they are very affectionate, and most specimens tame quickly. Their talking ability is excellent. Owners of red-heads say that they learn to imitate more quickly than many of the more common species, a high point in their favor. I have no information as to how they behave in aviaries or if they have been bred in captivity. I would think that breeding is likely if they are kept in a flighted aviary.

Now as to coloring! The crown, to the eyes and almost to the nape of the neck, is rich crimson red with a touch of soft lavender above the eyes, and just below the crimson cap. The cheeks are a pleasing shade of bright green, which of course sets off the cap and yellowish horn color of the beak. The rest of the body is green with a dark edge to the feathers, and there is some red and blue on the wings.

The female has less red on the crown and, as is common in this genus, a smaller bill.

CONURES

The members of the conure group vary widely in color, size and habitat, although all hail from the New World. Their main characteristics are large heads and beaks, long slender bodies and long tapering tails. They are similar to the macaws to which they are closely related. Although some are larger than the smallest macaws, conures can always be distinguished from macaws by their much smaller bare eye patch.

The majority of conures take kindly to cage life, becoming tame and affectionate household pets. With perseverance, young birds can be taught to repeat a few words, and in some cases they talk quite well. Because of the differences in individual birds, it is difficult to state which species makes the best talking pet. Since some varieties are more often imported than others, it is from these that the choice has to be made. Certain varieties are noisier than others, making them more suited to aviary life than to a cage.

Many species have been encouraged to nest in aviaries. On some occasions smaller species have nested and reared young in large cages. They are easy to feed and very hardy, which has added to their popularity among bird keepers.

They range in size from the greater Patagonian conure, which is some 20 inches long, to the small crimson-breasted conure, which is about nine inches.

Aztec Conure *(Aratinga astec)*
Also known as the olive-throated parakeet
Habitat: Mexico and Central America

This bird is sometimes confused with the Petz or half moon conure because it is about the same size and coloring, although the average Aztec is, if anything, a little larger. The overall color is green; the flights have a slate blue tinge. Throat and breast are brownish; belly is greenish yellow. The yellow cere has a bright orange spot in the center. The eyes too are yellow, encircled by bare white skin. The Aztec lacks the crescent of orange color on the forehead which distinguishes the half moon.

Golden-crowned Conure *(Aratinga aurea)*
Also known as peach-fronted conure
Habitat: Brazil, Paraguay and Bolivia

These are slightly larger than their near relative the Petz or half moon, which they resemble in color. The orange red on the head is very bright and covers the entire forehead and crown, whereas with the Petz only the forehead has the orange coloring. Also the beak of the golden-crowned is dark; that of the Petz is a light horn color. They are similar in habits and temperament and can be trained equally well.

Half Moon Conure *(Aratinga canicularis eburnirostrum)*
Also known as Petz conure

Habitat: Western Mexico, Central America

These popular little conures are some nine and a half inches long including four inches of tail. They are olive green in color, darker on the upper parts and yellowish on the lower. There is some dark blue on the flight feathers. The forehead has a band of orange red which deepens with age, and the crown is dull blue. It is the orange red on the heads which gives the birds their "half moon" name.

Young birds are easily trained. They quickly learn to perform tricks and pick up a few words. They are exceedingly hardy and relatively inexpensive.

Cuban Conure *(Aratinga euops)*
Also known as red-speckled conure or euops conure

Habitat: Cuba and Isle of Pines

These are smaller than the Wagler's conure but have the same two colors. The Cubans are a quite trainable species and their ten-inch size makes them easy to handle. Some specimens have been known to talk in voices that were quite clear.

The main color is green with bright scarlet red on crown, cheeks and on the under wing coverts. The wing butts are also speckled with red; the somewhat large beak is pale horn. Strangely enough, although these birds are plentiful at times, no breeding activity has to my knowledge been reported. They might make good subjects for anyone wanting to try.

Queen of Bavaria Conure *(Aratinga guarouba)*
Also known as golden parakeet or yellow conure

Habitat: Brazil

These are quite rare and among the most beautiful of all the conures. The overall color is a brilliant golden yellow with some bright green flight feathers, a color which distinguishes it from the majority of conures. Nearly 15 inches in length, they are powerfully built birds with large horn-colored beaks. The few specimens kept as pets have proved to be very tame and amenable, although I can find no record of their learning to talk.

Jandaya Conure *(Aratinga jandaya)*
Also known as yellow-headed conure or flaming parakeet

A pair of Jandaya conures **(Aratinga jandaya)**. *A Müller-Schmida photo.*

Habitat: Brazil

These popular conures are firm favorites with all who are fortunate enough to know them. Their size seems to vary between 10 inches and 12 inches. They tame very well and become most friendly with their owners. With training they make good talking pets. When excited or frightened their natural call becomes rather loud.

Their plumage is a mixture of very bright colors. The head, neck, throat and upper chest are a lovely rich golden yellow with a red orange suffusion above the beak and extending to the eyes and cheeks. There is also some red tinting on the chest, turning to deep red on the under-parts. The vent area and thighs are a dull green with some red flecking. The top of the tail is olive green in the middle, grading to dark blue and then black. The mantle, back and wings are bright green, and the flights have some blue shading. The rump is also green but with some red intermixed. The extent of the yellow and red areas on individual birds varies according to age. Hen birds do not usually carry such bright reds and yellows as the cocks.

Jandayas are easy to keep and feed. They have proved themselves to be really good breeders in captivity. Owners of breeding pairs claim that they make excellent parents and take good care of their young.

Brown-eared Conure *(Aratinga pertinax ocularis)*

Habitat: Panama

This small species is about nine inches long including its fairly long tail. Although they are not brilliantly colored, they have a warm and friendly nature which recommends them as pets. Their general color is green, darkly toned on the upper parts, paler on the underparts. The forehead and crown have a strong bluish wash, and the face, cheeks and throat are brown with yellowish feathers in the middle. The flight feathers are dark with a blue suffusion. The beak is dark horn. This is a most pleasing species.

Sun Conure *(Aratinga solstitialis)*

Also known as yellow conure

Habitat: Guianas, Venezuela

This beautifully colored species rivals the Queen of Bavaria conure for richness of color, but it is a little smaller. The general color is a bright yellow orange, with the wings and tail green tinted with blue on the outer edges and tips. These colors make them a much sought after species.

Although quite rare, a few pairs are occasionally seen in collections. Like Jandayas they are good breeders. They have also been crossed with other species of conures, and hybrids have been reared on several occasions. With perseverance it should be possible to establish aviary breeding strains of these golden yellow conures.

Wagler's Conure *(Aratinga wagleri)*

Also known as red-fronted conure or scarlet-fronted parakeet

Habitat: Venezuela, Colombia and Ecuador

This is a mainly green and red species of some 14 inches overall length. There are several subspecies with slight differences in coloring. At the present time Wagler's are not seen too often, but at one period they were in collections all over the world. Most specimens are docile and become tame and friendly toward their owners. Their voices are rather harsh but fortunately are not used frequently. They can be persuaded to imitate a few words. I know of only one attempt at breeding them. Eggs were laid but not hatched.

The general color is green, lighter on the upper parts, deeper and richer on the underparts. The forehead and crown are deep red, and this extends in flecking down the throat. The red is emphasized by the pale horn color of their beaks.

Weddel's Conure *(Aratinga weddellii)*

Also known as the dusky-headed parakeet

Red and green are the predominant colors of the Wagler's conure (Aratinga wagleri). Photo by L. van der Meid.

Habitat: Northwestern South America and the Amazon Basin

This 12-inch conure was once considered quite rare, probably because the collectors did not cover all the area it inhabits in the western Amazon basin. It ranges from northern Peru to Ecuador and north into Colombia, where it is apparently more plentiful than in the more southern part of its range in Brazil.

The overall plumage is green. The entire head is a brownish gray tinged on top with blue. The flights and tips of the tail feathers are ultramarine blue, the underside of the wings and tail black. It is a bird with a quiet beauty all its own.

Nanday Conure *(Nandayus nenday)*

Also known as black-hooded parakeet

Habitat: Bolivia, Brazil and Paraguay

This very popular conure is some 12 inches in overall length with a long slender tail. Their color scheme of green, red and black is most attractive, and they always command attention either as single pets or aviary pairs. By nature they are quite gentle except, of course, at breeding time, when they may become a little pugnacious. They are consistent and regular breeders, and in some establishments they have been bred for many generations. Good parents, they rear their chicks without fuss or trouble. As far as I know they do not have any vices.

The head and beak are shining black, with the ear area green. Some of the wing feathers are a deep blue-black. The tail is bluish green and the underside is black, with the general color of the birds being bright green, deep on the underparts, more bluish on the breast. The thighs are a delightful rich bright red accentuated by the black legs and feet.

They eat the usual parrot seed mixture and are particularly partial to various seeding grasses, green foods and fresh fruits.

Taken all in all, the nanday is a most desirable species. When breeding they take well to the conventional type of nesting box, but they do not like to be disturbed.

White-eared Conure *(Pyrrhura leucotis)*

Also known as maroon-faced parakeet

Habitat: Venezuela, Brazil

These are among the smallest members of the large conure group, but they have one of the best color combinations. They make excellent pets and are quite consistent breeders. They have also been successfully crossed with several other species of conures. It would seem that white-ears breed quite well in small flighted aviaries, making very good parents. As pets in the house they are calm and gentle and will repeat a few odd words, but they never become first-rate talkers.

Their color is varied, with the upper wings, flanks and vent area a dark green with a rich maroon patch over the rump. The tail is dark on top with a strong brownish maroon shading in places, and the underparts are brownish red encircled by green. The beak is black and the head brown with the ear coverts white, hence the name. The collar is bluish, the lores bright maroon with the chest green and the feathers scalloped with buff and black at the tips. The sexes are alike in color, but the fully adult males have broader heads and are more aggressive than the hens.

Some years ago on a Sunday morning in late August, I visited a fellow bird breeder in the next town. One of the purposes of the visit was to look at a consignment of South American birds he had just received. On arrival I was proudly shown a magnificent pair of hyacinthine macaws, a fine pair of blue-fronted amazons and a nice collection of conures. Among them was an odd white-eared conure whose companion had died on the journey to England. It seemed a friendly little thing, but rather lonely and out of place among all the other couples. I asked to buy the bird, as I have a weakness for odd specimens, and was delighted when my offer was accepted.

The following spring I noticed that the white-eared was behaving with all the characteristics of a cock bird, so I started looking around for a mate. For several weeks my quest was unsuccessful; then I saw an advertisement in a bird paper offering a pair. I tried to buy the hen only, but the owner would sell them only as a pair, so I bought them. As I knew that both sexes of white-eareds are the same color, I decided that the bird with the slighter build was the hen. I then put my cock and the new hen in one of my flighted parakeet aviaries together with a log-type nest box. My selection was correct, as before long the pair was busy playing around the nest box, happy in each other's company.

In due course the hen started to spend a lot of her day in the nest box, and I had high hopes of seeing some eggs soon. About a week later as I was feeding my birds I heard a lot of noise coming from the white-eared conures' aviary. On investigating I found the little hen stretched on the floor under the nest box from where she had fallen, and her mate calling loudly for help. I picked up the hen; she was alive but suffering badly from egg binding. I put her in my hospital cage with the temperature set 85°F (30°C). The heat treatment was successful, and she laid a soft-shelled egg that evening although she seemed very weak and unsteady on her feet. I looked into her nest box and found that she had already laid two eggs which had been broken in her struggles to pass the soft-shelled egg.

During this time her lonely mate was most distressed and continually calling, so I thought that the best way to quiet him was to put the other white-eared cock in the aviary with him. For a few days they treated each other with great respect and then settled down in friendly fashion. As the little hen slowly recovered she became extremely tame, so I decided to find a home for her as a household pet. This I did, and she made her new owner and family happy for many years.

I did not take much notice of the two white-eared cocks beyond seeing that they had their proper food and attention and that they were both healthy. Early one hot September afternoon I heard a scrappy noise coming from the nest box in the white-eared conures' aviary. I at once suspected field mice and went into the aviary prepared to deal with them. Quietly opening the top of the box, I peered inside and to my utter amazement saw two chicks about three weeks old. I hastily closed the lid and stepped quickly out of the flight so as not to disturb the parent birds. The "pair" I had bought were in fact both hens, one more robust than the other. I was, of course, delighted with my good fortune and very happy a few weeks later when two youngsters flew from the nest.

In bird breeding it is often a series of circumstances like these that lead to an unexpected breeding success.

MACAWS

Mention the name macaw and immediately one mentally conjures up

A blue and yellow macaw showing off one of its tricks. Photo by K. Donnelly.

Close-up of a blue and yellow macaw **(Ara ararauna)**. *Photo by K. Donnelly.*

a great brilliantly colored parrot with a long tail and gaudy plumage. Nature really ran riot when she colored these tremendous birds; they range in size from 13 inches to three feet. None are found in the Old World—they all come from tropical America.

If taken from the nest and hand-tamed, macaws become tremendously playful and friendly pets despite their somewhat formidable beaks. That they can be taught tricks is evident from the number that appear in bird acts. Older birds, although they can be amenable, never really become as friendly with human beings as do the young ones. Their vocabulary is seldom extensive, but the words they do utter are usually clear and easily understood.

In an aviary—and it must be an extremely strong and well-built structure—macaws look truly magnificent. Although they are not free breeders, when a good true pair is obtained and given suitable accommodations they will continue to rear families for years.

The owner's idea of the right mate for a particular bird is sometimes wrong, as the following incident proves. A large breeder of parrots had in his extensive collection several blue and yellow macaws—two fine cocks, one very nice hen and another nondescript hen. The better hen was housed with the best cock bird, but although the pair got on together quite well, nothing happened in spite of the cock's persistent attempt to invite the hen into the nesting box. One day the cock bird found a loose piece of wiring and made his escape. After flying around the estate he returned to another, smaller aviary which housed the nondescript hen. Through the wires they became quite friendly. The owner, on seeing this, caged the hen, opened the door and in strutted the cock. Being a wise man, the breeder thought this natural selection might be fruitful, so he provided the birds with a suitable nesting box. Almost immediately the hen was inside, and in due course eggs were laid and beautiful chicks reared. This went on for several seasons, and quite a collection of aviary-bred macaws accumulated from this pair. The very fine hen was tried with several other cock birds but to no avail. It only goes to show that selective breeding does not always pay off.

The intelligence of macaws is demonstrated by the fact that many parks and zoological gardens have trained them to fly freely about the grounds and return voluntarily to their quarters at night. When several species of them are given this freedom together they frequently interbreed. For example, the blue and gold macaw will cross with the scarlet to produce a hybrid which resembles the blue and gold, but with a bright red-orange chest. The military also crosses freely with the scarlet, and their offspring is intermediate; the red brow is maintained, the chest is reddish green and the rest of the plumage is intermediate. These hybrids are fertile and can be bred with each other or back to the parent stock.

Hyacinthine Macaw *(Anodorhynchus hyacinthinus)*

Habitat: Paraguay, Brazil

These hardy macaws, commonly called hyacinth macaws, measure somewhere around 34 inches in length, two feet of which are taken up by their tapering tails. Hyacinths are frequently acclaimed as the most beautifully colored of all the macaws. Their coloring is a deep hyacinth blue throughout. Their exeptionally large curved beaks are of a dark horn color, and the naked skin around their eyes and the base of their beak is a strong yellow which sets off the body color.

I know many owners of these handsome birds, and they all agree that the birds are extremely gentle and affectionate. Usually they are not especially noisy, but if they become overexcited or upset they can most certainly raise their voices. Because of their rarity, hyacinths are quite expensive.

Indigo Macaw *(Anodorhynchus leari)*

Also known as Lear's macaw

Habitat: Brazil

These macaws are similar to the hyacinthine but smaller, being about

Indigo macaw ***(Anodorhynchus leari)***. *Photo by L. van der Meid.*

30 inches overall. Their coloring is blue but not the brilliant blue of the hyacinthine. Their beaks are dark and their bare eye skin a dull yellow. These macaws are not often imported, but those who own them always speak well of their hardiness and extreme playfulness. Another member of this genus is the glaucous macaw *(Anodorhynchus glaucus)*, which is slightly larger than the indigo with a more greenish brown tone.

Blue and Yellow Macaw *(Ara ararauna)*

Habitat: Northern South America

This is an extremely popular macaw. There are probably more of them in captivity than any other species. Just over 30 inches long, they are mainly blue in color with yellow on their underparts. This is set off by a white face lined with black, which gives them a fascinating look. This species has been bred in captivity. They make very fine pets, being amenable and easy to handle but, as with all parrots, much depends on their early training and treatment. I recommend them highly.

Illiger's Macaw *(Ara maracana)*

Habitat: Paraguay, Brazil

This is a very small species only some 16 to 18 inches in overall length. They are dark in color with some patches of red on the underparts and orange red on the forehead. Illiger's macaws have been successfully bred in captivity, and I believe that on several occasions second generations have been bred.

I have a rather interesting story to tell of one of these successes. It happened a few years ago in the aviaries of an amateur but expert parrot keeper. It all began one summer's day when a friend left an Illiger's macaw in his care while he went on holiday. As it happened, the holiday turned out to be one of several months, and during this time the keeper became very attached to the macaw. It was his first experience with this species and he was impressed with its gentleness and tameness. When the owner on his return was told how good the bird had been and how attached his friend had become to it, he made him a present of the macaw.

The Illiger's was installed in a spare parrot aviary together with a pair of silver pheasants, and they all got on together extremely well. The following summer he had the opportunity to buy another Illiger's, which he installed with his gift bird and the pheasants. He had no idea as to the sex of either bird, but as time went on it became evident that they were a true pair. This, of course, induced him to buy a large nesting box (one of the grandfather's clock kind) and to install it in the

Illiger's macaws aviary, which still contained the silver pheasants (which had by this time reared several families of their own). The Illiger's macaws at once investigated the nesting box and had a fine time 'going in and out of the nest hole, which they proceeded to enlarge considerably. After a period one of the birds disappeared and all was quiet, with the other one sitting on sentry duty on top of the box. After about five weeks the owner could wait no longer. He had to look into the nest box. There he found the hen sitting quite happily on four lovely white eggs, but alas they were all clear (infertile).

The following year the birds tried again. Again four eggs were laid and this time three were fertile. To his delight all three hatched into healthy chicks. After about five anxious weeks the first of the babies made its appearance at the top of the nesting box, and within a few days all five birds were sitting in a line on a perch in the aviary. What a wonderful sight they made and how very proud the parents were.

During the time they were rearing their young, the adults' food consisted of the usual mixture of canary seed, white millet, sunflower, a little hemp and buckwheat and a few peanuts, together with fresh fruit and plenty of sprouting grasses, chickweed, sow thistle heads, and, of course, mixed grit and cuttlebone.

Red and Green Macaw (Ara chloroptera)

Also known as maroon macaw, red and blue macaw or green-winged macaw

Habitat: Northern South America into Central America

This widely kept species is slightly shorter in overall length (34 inches) than the red and yellow. Their red is a lovely crimson hue, and their blue, rich and deep, at times shades into dark green on the wings. The bare skin areas are light and marked with tiny red feathers which add to their quaintness.

Most specimens are good-natured and get on well with animals and children, which makes them highly acceptable as household pets—but here again the best results are obtained by taming the birds when they are young.

Red and Yellow Macaw (Ara macao)

Also known as scarlet macaw

Habitat: Central America, Mexico

These are several inches longer than the red and green macaw, with the extra length being made up mostly of tail. Their color pattern is red, yellow and blue, with the naked eye skin showing a distinct pinkish tone. The beak is horn-colored on top and dark underneath.

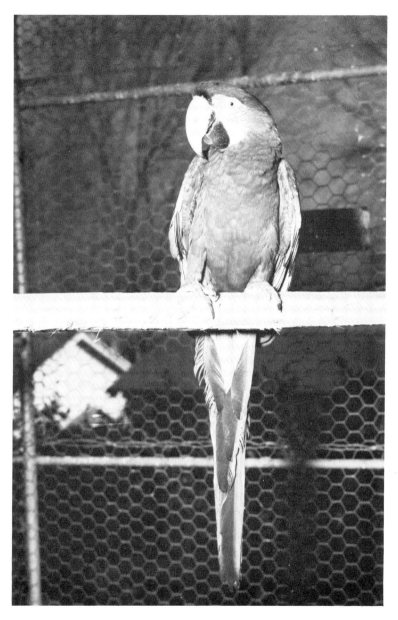

A red and green macaw **(Ara chloroptera)** *is another well known and well liked macaw. Photo by L. van der Meid.*

Opinion as to their friendliness seems to differ, but I think this can be accounted for by the fact that various birds have had different initial training. The ones I have known have, without exception, been most friendly and placid types.

Military Macaw *(Ara militaris)*
Also known as green macaw

Habitat: Northern South America and Mexico

The predominant color is olive green. Their beaks are dark, and their heads are a mixture of dark red and blue. The flight feathers, rump underparts and tail are also blue, with the upper part of the tail red. Most specimens are easy to handle and make excellent pets. The average length is about 27 inches, the female being a little smaller.

Noble Macaw *(Ara nobilis)*
Also known as Hahn's macaw

Habitat: Northern South America and Trinidad

These are the smallest macaws, being only 12 inches long, smaller than some of the larger conures, which they resemble except for the bare facial area characteristic of all macaws. Their main coloring is grass green, with bright scarlet on wing coverts and underparts and a bluish tinge on the forehead. The beak is black. The underside of the tail is golden yellow.

These birds are not seen too often in captivity even though they are small enough to be kept in much smaller aviaries than their larger cousins. I have only known one Hahn's that was kept as a pet. He was most friendly but could only repeat one word, his name—Joey!!

Chestnut-fronted Macaw *(Ara severa)*
Also known as severe macaw

These are small macaws some 14 inches long. Their main color is green with a bluish tone on the head, red wing coverts and green underparts. These are pleasant birds and, being relatively small, make excellent household pets. With perseverance, they become extremely tame and even learn to say a few words, but like all other macaws their ability to imitate the human voice is limited.

Little Blue Macaw *(Cyanopsitta spixii)*
Also known as Spix's macaw

Habitat: Eastern Brazil

This bird is silvery gray blue and is about 22 inches long, with the unusual feature of the eye skin being dark whereas in most species it is light. These macaws are rare in captivity.

PARAKEETS AND OTHER AMERICAN PARROTS
Lineolated Parakeet *(Bolborhynchus lineola)*
Also called barred parakeet

Habitat: Southern Mexico through Central America and northern South America

The general feathering is of varying shades of green, paler on the breast, brighter on the forehead and more olive green on the back and flanks. The plumage, except in the middle of the breast, is barred with black that is heaviest on the back. There are black bars on each wing, and the feathers of the rump are tipped with black. The short tail feathers are sharply pointed, green, with black along the shaft. Total length is six and three-fourths inches. The female is stockier than the male, the green areas of her plumage are less brilliant, her tail is all green and the markings are less distinct. The immature birds are even paler than the female.

Here we have a lovely, playful little bird that is not too expensive and is easy to maintain. It also breeds well in captivity. Lineolateds are sensitive to cold, so they should never be exposed to low temperatures. Those who own them are constantly reporting on their amusing antics.

Tui Parakeets *(Brotogeris sanctithomae)*
Habitat: Ecuador, Peru

These delightful little parakeets, only about six and a half inches long, are pleasing in temperament and easy to train and handle. Again the color is mainly green, with the underparts and rump a paler tone. The forehead and center of the crown are bright yellow with a stripe of yellow behind each eye and the surrounding area washed with blue. There is also some blue shading on the wings. The beak, a shade of dark horn, is set off by the yellow of the forehead.

Bee Bee Parakeet *(Brotogeris jugularis)*
Also known as orange-chinned parakeet

Habitat: Venezuela, Colombia

This popular species averages about seven inches in length. Like most of their group, they quickly settle down and become tame and friendly with their owners. Their talking abilities are somewhat limited, but the voice is clear and quite loud. They have been bred in aviaries and cages and have also produced hybrids with related species on several occasions.

Their coloring is green, darker above and becoming paler on the underparts. The wings are green with some brown, and there is blue on the flight feathers. The beak is horn-colored, and there is a bright orange patch under the chin which gives them their alternative name. Both sexes are alike in color, with the cock birds a little more sturdy in build. The behavior of the parent birds when nesting has not, as far as I know, been recorded.

When first imported they must be kept warm until they get used to the local climate. Their main diet is canary seed with some hemp and sunflower, a few millet sprays and of course plenty of fruit. They like a shelter in which to sleep and should be given an old nest box or a chunk of hollow log.

White-winged Parakeet *(Brotogeris versicolorus versicolorus)*
Habitat: South America

These nine-inch parakeets are friendly and easy to tame. The color is green, very rich at the top and yellowish below. The front parts of the head and face have a strong bluish gray wash. The outer flight feathers are black with a lot of blue at the edges and tips, then blue and green with the remainder and the secondaries white, slightly tinted in places with yellow. The major wing coverts are yellow, and the beak is light horn. Since both sexes are alike in color they are difficult to distinguish, but this is not important unless they are to be bred.

Notice the seed mixture offered to this canary-winged parakeet **(Brotogeris versicolorus chiriri).** *Photo by Dr. H. R. Axelrod.*

Canary-winged Parakeet *(Brotogeris versicolorus chiriri)*
Also known as golden-winged parakeet

Habitat: South America

This bird is fast competing for popularity with its smaller "rivals," the tui and bee bee parakeets. It is about nine inches long, but a good half of this length is tail.

The basic plumage is green, darker above and lighter on the breast. There is some blue on the wings. The dark flights are broken by a narrow yellow band, hence the name. The sexes are identical in color and markings, but the male is slightly bulkier and has a broader head.

While the canary-winged does not learn to speak too well, it does develop amusing little habits that endear it to its owners. It seems to have more intelligence than the average parakeet, and it can be easily tamed, although it is inclined to be a bit raucous.

Canary-wings seem to be quite hardy once acclimated. They like to sleep in the shelter of a box. Although they have been bred in captivity, they are far from being easy breeders. Canary-winged parakeets are good subjects for the newcomer to the fancy. They are not too spectacular in color, but they are hardy and affectionate.

Quaker Parakeet *(Myiopsitta monachus)*
Also known as monk parakeet

Habitat: South America

This is a medium size, almost all green-backed bird. The unusual charm of their coloring is the face, throat and breast, which have a soft quaker gray appearance. The feather edges are distinct, giving the gray area a scaled appearance. There is a suffusion of yellow on the thighs and underparts. Quakers are reasonably quiet and, consequently, make easily trained pets who will quickly learn to say a few words.

They differ from the majority of parrots in that they actually build nests of sticks and twigs, whereas the vast majority of the family nest in hollow tree trunks. To breed in aviaries they must be supplied with quantities of freshly cut twigs and coarse vegetation to use in building their rather untidy nests.

Because the quaker deviates from other parrots (except lovebirds) in its nest-building proclivity, it has engendered a great deal of speculation. One Victorian lady, perhaps more poetically than scientifically, rhapsodized thus:

> I, though a Parrot, find that as I live in bogs and marshes, the trunks of trees and branches are apt to be damp, and my young to be drowned by a sudden rising of the waters, therefore I will build on trees, and since I am good

tempered and sociable, I will join my sisters for our common protection from enemies; and since I do not want to climb, I will carry up sticks in my beak, and I will line my nest with soft grass for health.

W.T. Greene has this to say about the species' name:

"Quaker?" Why are these birds called by the popular designation of the estimable people who name themselves "Friends"? It is difficult to say; but possibly on account of the fact that the head, throat and breast of these birds is of that delicate pearly shade of grey, so often affected by the lady members of that Society; but there the resemblance ceases, for the remainder of the plumage is bright grass green excepting the flight feathers, which are blue.

Hawk-headed Parrot *(Deroptyus accipitrinus)*

Also known as the hawk-headed caique

Habitat: Northern South America

This is a striking looking species some 14 inches in length. They are mainly brown striped with buff coloring on the head. Their breast color is reddish edged with blue, and the nape and back of head feathers are red broadly edged with blue. These feathers are erected when the bird is excited and form a sort of headdress or halo, giving the bird an unusually exotic appearance like a bird of prey. The rest of the body is a dull green. Owners of these strange-looking birds say that in spite of their appearance they tame reasonably well and take kindly to captive conditions. They have been known to repeat a few words and noises.

Bronze-winged Parrot *(Pionus chalcopterus)*

Habitat: Andes of Colombia, Ecuador and northwestern Peru

These are relatively rare, but specimens do appear on the market from time to time. Like the white-crowned parrots they are difficult to sex, and owners of single birds often do not know their pet's sex. As far as I know there are no records of these delightful birds having bred in captivity. They have pleasing natures, quickly become tame and confiding and seem to take kindly to captivity. This being so, I feel that a true pair of bronze-winged parrots would, if given the opportunity in a suitable aviary, make a definite attempt to breed. A few specimens have been known to say an occasional word or two. The crown, cheek area, back of head and upper neck are of a dark bluish green. The wings are a brownish bronze. The tail and upper parts of the breast are an extremely dark blue, with the lower parts an irregular patterning of reddish pink and bluff. The tail is dark blue with the under coverts orange red,

*Bronze-winged parrots (**Pionus chalcopterus**). The ones shown are not yet mature birds. Photo by R. Van Nostrand, San Diego Zoo.*

and the vent area is red. The rump is also dark blue, and the area between the legs is bright violet. This rainbow of colors is set off by the yellowish horn of the beak.

Violet Parrot *(Pionus fuscus)*
Also known as dusky parrot

Habitat: Lower Amazon areas, Venezuela and the Guianas

The violet parrot is just over ten inches long and is built on lines similar to the African grey. The top of the head is a dull bluish shade with red just above the nostrils. Dark patches at the ear coverts fade to pale buff. The back is dark brown with pinkish feather edges. The chest is grayish, becoming a rich wine color along the sides. The under tail coverts are deep purplish red, and the tail itself is a bright violet, becoming very deep at the base. These are amusing parrots that become extremely tame with a little attention; they love to play like kittens. They are hardy, and although I have no records of breeding at hand I know they have made attempts to nest in some avairies. They can be likened to the Senegal parrot. All the specimens I have known have learned to repeat a few words, but in a peculiar high-pitched voice.

Blue-headed Parrot *(Pionus menstruus)*

Also known as the red-vented parrot

Habitat: Costa Rica to Bolivia and Brazil

In overall size (length about 11 inches) and body type the blue-headed parrot resembles a small amazon. Its distinguishing feature is, obviously, its violet-blue head, neck, throat and breast. The rest of the body is a dark grass green, while its wings are an olive-green reflecting bronze in certain lights. The ear coverts are black, while the under tail coverts and vent are a fiery red. The tail itself is dark green edged with blue. The beak is horn-colored with a pink spot at the base of the upper mandible. Legs are a greenish white and the claws black. The female resembles the male, except that the blue is less pronounced and she has a smaller, narrower beak.

This is a truly beautiful bird, and those who know it well claim that it is quieter than most parrots and an extremely affectionate pet. Its feeding and maintenance is the same as the amazons'.

White-crowned Parrot *(Pionus senilis)*

Also known as the white-capped parrot

Habitat: Central America and tropical Mexico

This unusually colored member of the Pionus group is just over nine inches long. The white areas on their heads give the birds their common name. Parrots with white in their plumage are not common, and this feature certainly makes them most desirable acquisitions. A few pairs have been kept in breeding aviaries, but I have not yet received any actual reports of breeding success.

Their ability to mimic the human voice is believed to be limited, but they have a gentle and most confiding nature that makes them most desirable as pets. The crown, chin and throat are pure white, with the breast a dark dull purplish blue. The cheeks and back of neck are a dark dull green with some bluish edging. Their wings are shaded green-bronze and scalloped with blue, and the under tail coverts are purplish red. The bare skin that surrounds the orange-colored eyes has a reddish flush. The sexes are colored alike, the only difference being in some cases that the cocks have a broader head.

Celestial Parrotlet *(Forpus coelestis)*

Also known as Lesson's or Pacific parrotlet

Habitat: Pacific slopes of Ecuador and Peru

This tiny parrotlet (about four inches long) is said to be quite common in its native habitat, but it is not seen in captivity too often. The male's head and face are a vivid green, while the back of the head is a

Celestial parrotlets, **Forpus coelestis** *(left) and turquoise-rumped parrotlets,* **F. cyanopygius** *(right). Photos by L. van der Meid.*

bluish gray fading into greenish; the lower back and rump are dark blue, as are the wing coverts. The tail is green, but the coverts have a bluish tinge and there is a blue streak behind the eye. The female is even smaller. She has no blue on the wings, and her breast and underparts are yellowish.

Experienced breeders claim that the celestials breed readily in captivity, but because of their aggressiveness during the mating season they should not be bred in colony flights.

Turquoise-rumped Parrotlet *(Forpus cyanopygius)*
Also known as Mexican parrotlet
Habitat: Western Mexico

The overall color is a green that is paler on the breast and cheeks. There is turquoise blue on the rump, lower back, lower edge of the wings and under wing coverts. Yellow-green marks the forehead and face. The female has none of the blue. Total length is about five inches.

Green-rumped Parrotlet *(Forpus passerinus)*
Habitat: Venezuela to Guianas and Brazil

Mainly green, but the green on the nape has a grayish tinge. The rump is a bright emerald green. There is pale blue on the wings and dark blue on the under wing coverts. The female lacks the blue. Reaches a length of five and a half inches.

White-bellied Caique *(Pionites leucogaster)*

Habitat: Amazon basin

These are more frequently imported than the black-headed caique, are of similar size and temperament and require the same care. The top of their heads down to their shoulders is a lovely apricot orange shade, with the sides of their face and throat yellow. All the upper parts from the shoulders down are a bright clear green. The thighs are also green but of a darker shade, with the under tail coverts yellow. Young birds may show some black on the crown which later turns to apricot.

Black-headed Caique *(Pionites melanocephala)*

Habitat: Northern South America

These interesting parrots are usually just over nine inches in length. They are colorful birds with large beaks. The top of the head is black with green below the eyes and on the back and wings. The middle of the breast is white, and a collar at the nape of the neck is yellowish. The cheeks are washed with golden yellow. The thighs, lower flanks and undertail coverts are an orange yellow. Not enough caiques have been kept in captivity to form a distinctive view of their suitability, although they do become tame and friendly and will, with perseverance, learn to repeat a few words. Caiques are, in my opinion, more suitable as aviary birds than as cage pets.

*Black-headed caique (**Pionites melanocephala**). Photo by L. van der Meid.*

*A large crest and enormous beak create an impression of ferocity in the great black cockatoo (**Probosciger atterimus**). However, it is considered to be a good-natured bird by breeders. Photo by F. M. Gorman.*

III   Australasian Parrots: Indonesia to Australia and the Pacific Islands

COCKATOOS

Whether the cockatoos or the macaws are more spectacular parrots is a subject of long debate that has never been resolved. The cockatoos have magnificent crests in their favor, while the macaws have their flamboyant tails.

The cockatoos make up a group of some 17 species with many subspecies. Most of them come from Australia, with a few from Indonesia and other areas in that part of the Pacific. None of them are found in the New World. They are heavily built birds, and all have erectile crests which they can keep flat on their heads or fan open at will. Their size varies widely from a foot to 30 inches. Most of the species are basically white; a few are black or dusty gray, but all of them have at least some touches of another color, usually varying shades of orange, red or yellow.

In general, they quickly become tame and friendly, but they are inclined to be noisy when excited or frightened. In general—although there are exceptions—they seldom develop very extensive vocabularies, and when they do talk, they inject extraneous noises into their conversations. But this does not keep them from repeating the words they do know over and over. While talking they are given to acrobatic displays and dancing, and this of course adds to their attraction as pets. They quickly make friends with dogs and cats and have in many cases been trained to perform with them.

Once acclimated, cockatoos are hardy birds who live extremely long lives—there are unsubstantiated claims of over a hundred years— and are passed down in families from generation to generation. They thrive well on a simple diet. They will nest in captivity, but not unless they have large flighted aviaries and tree hollows in which to lay their eggs.

Cockatoos have the unique habit of "powdering" themselves with a dust produced by the feathers. This powder, which gives them a mealy satiny look, helps to keep the feathers waterproof and, some say, vermin-free.

Gang Gang Cockatoo *(Callocephalon fimbriatum)*
Also known as red-crowned cockatoo or red-helmeted cockatoo

These are perhaps the smallest of the dark cockatoos, being only about 13½ inches long, slightly less than the roseate cockatoo. It is unfortunate that these little cockatoos are so difficult to obtain, as they are quite different from the others in the group.

Their general coloring is a soft dove gray, but each feather has a light tip that gives a scalloped appearance. The medium length tail and flights are a darker gray, as is the beak. The outstanding feature is the head, which in the male is flaming red topped with a large crest of soft, curved feathers. In fact, their scientific name means "beautifully fringed head." The lower part of the stomach is barred with orange, red and white in the male birds. The females have the same area with dull orange and white suffused with green. The females, alas, lack the lovely scarlet red crown. Theirs is gray.

Gang gang cockatoos make very good birds for either aviaries or as cage birds and quickly become friendly and tame. I have no personal knowledge of their vocal abilities.

Funereal Cockatoo *(Calyptorhynchus funereus)*
Also known as yellow-tailed black cockatoo
Habitat: Australia

These represent the more somber side of the cockatoo group. When fully adult they are some 26 inches long. Their overall coloring is on the dull side, but they have certain rather attractive features. Their upper parts are black with a brownish tinting and a little glossy in appearance. The underparts are blackish with the feathers lightly tipped with a pale yellow shade. The tail is dark but carries a yellow band flecked with dark brown spots. The lemon yellow ear or cheek patches cover an extensive area, and the feathering is very fine, giving an almost hair-like appearance. The hen birds show much more yellow on their feather tips.

Banksian Red-tailed Cockatoo *(Calyptorhynchus magnificus)*
Also known as the red-tailed black cockatoo
Habitat: Australia
Banksians range in size from 24 to 27 inches. Their general coloring is a dull black with a grayish tinge on the breast. The tail has a band of orange red, and their crest, when erected, suggests a Roman helmet. The female's head and underparts are marked with yellow.

White-crested Cockatoo *(Cacatua alba)*
Also known as greater white-crested cockatoo or umbrella crested cockatoo
Habitat: Australia
These large birds are slightly less long than the Moluccan cockatoo and are entirely white, including their crests. Their beaks are black, and the naked skin surrounding their eyes is tinted blue. These two areas of color stand out strongly, making the birds look very attractive. Most white-crested cockatoos are excellent talkers and will chatter away for hours on end, but as with all of these birds the best results are obtained when they are taken into training when young.

Great Sulphur-crested Cockatoo *(Cacatua galerita)*
Habitat: Australia and New Guinea
These are probably the best known of the cockatoos. They are very common in their native land. The greater is some 20 inches long; the similar lesser measures 13 inches. The long crest and sometimes the ear coverts are lemon or sulphur yellow. The black beaks contrast sharply with the bird's basically white plumage. In spite of their great size, relatively powerful bills and raucous voices, the owners of these birds speak affectionately of their gentleness with both human beings and other birds. They have been known to form very strong attachments to smaller members of the parrot family. Generally speaking, they make satisfactory pets and can be expected to live very long lives.

Lesser Sulphur-crested Cockatoo *(Cacatua sulphurea)*

Habitat: Indonesia and Celebes

In appearance this is a smaller version of the greater sulphur-crested, although its white has more yellow tinges.

Leadbeater's Cockatoo *(Cacatua leadbeateri)*

Also known as the Major Mitchell cockatoo and the pink cockatoo

Habitat: Australia

If you'll excuse the pun, no other cockatoo can top the Leadbeater's crest. When fully erect, it fans out into bands of white, red and yellow. The body color is white, but it is a white suffused with a soft rosy shade that is heavier on the neck, chin and breast. The eye skin and beak are light. The sexes are alike in plumage, but the female's eyes are always reddish brown, while the male's are black.

Compared with the other cockatoos, these birds are of medium size, neither too large nor too small—about 16 inches. They will quickly learn a limited number of words and become so tame that an owner can do almost anything with his pet. They have been known to form friendships with all kinds of animals from kittens to horses.

Under the right conditions, leadbeater's cockatoos will nest and rear young in captivity. They have the reputation of being excellent parents.

Moluccan Cockatoo *(Cacatua moluccensis)*

Also known as salmon-crested cockatoo, rose-crested cockatoo and red-crested cockatoo

Habitat: Indonesia

Greene agrees with Karl Russ that this magnificent bird is one of the handsomest of them all. He comments:

> Surpassing in size of body the largest of the Macaws, and covered with feathers that remind one of childhood in the country and raspberries and cream, it is no wonder this monarch of the Cockatoo race has had admirers from the earliest day of its importation into Europe, almost a couple of centuries ago.
>
> It is a large bird, measuring 17 to 18 inches in length, of which the tail occupies about six; the wings are each about a foot long, and very powerful, so that the bird when wild has great capacity for flight; often soaring at such an elevation that it is invisible to the naked eye, although its piercing cries are distinctly audible as it flies to and fro between its feeding and its sleeping grounds.

The Moluccan cockatoo **(Cacatua moluccensis)** *is greatly favored by many trainers for performing tricks for entertainment. Photo by K. Donnelly.*

White, tinged with pale rose red, is the prevailing colour of the plumage, which in a perfect specimen is powdered copiously with a substance resembling French chalk in appearance, that adds a wonderful luster to the coat. The crest, which is about six inches in length, lies down the back of the head and upper part of the neck, and is scarcely noticed until the bird, getting excited from whatever cause, lifts it up and displays not only the length and width of the plumes that compose it, but their beautiful ruddy orange tint. The side tail feathers have their inner webs a pale primrose yellow, from base to center, the remaining portion, as well as the central pair, being white. The beak is bluish black, the circle of the eyes pearl grey, and the eyes themselves deep hazel, although some individuals have them of a darker shade than others, and these may be the males.

The Moluccan cockatoo, like other large parrots, can make good use of its zygodactylous feet to grasp foods and other objects. Photo by Dr. A. E. Decoteau.

Roseate Cockatoo *(Eolophus roseicapillus)*

Also known as rose-breasted cockatoo or galah cockatoo

Habitat: Australia

These relatively small cockatoos are about 14 inches long. Their color is a neat mixture of white, soft gray and a deep rosy pink. Their crests usually lie flat on their heads, but when erected they too show the deep pink coloring. The underparts, chest and throat are a soft shade of rosy pink, and the upper parts, wings and tail are a soft dove gray, with the tails being a little darker than the rest of the body.

As a general rule, they are very friendly birds that become attached to each other and to their owners. Unfortunately their talking ability is limited, but it is compensated for by their great capacity for friendship.

There are many galahs which spend almost all of their time at liberty. When free they must be watched to see that they do not damage furniture or woodwork. Of all the cockatoos, they are the easiest to breed and many galah babies are reared every year; in some instances many generations have been bred. Let me tell you the story of one such breeding.

It all began with a little girl calling out to her mother that their pet galah, Joey, had laid an egg. Mother came rushing in to see the phenomenon, and sure enough, there was a small white oval egg at one corner of Joey's cage and the bird was eyeing it in wonderment. The family argued as to whether or not someone had slipped another bird's egg into the cage as a joke. In two days this suggestion was dispelled as another egg appeared beside the first and Joey started to sit proudly upon them. By the end or the week there were four neat little oval white eggs in the cage corner. The family had owned Joey for some four years and had always been of the opinion that she was a "he"—hence the name!

After some inquiries the father discovered that the color of both sexes in roseate cockatoos was the same. He also found that this particular species had been bred in captivity on quite a number of occasions and that, generally speaking, they were kind and attentive parents when given the opportunity to nest. It was decided that Joey should have a mate and that a special little house be constructed for the pair. Some few weeks later the new bird, a known male, was introduced to his future wife. Roseate cockatoos are very lovable little birds and become much attached to each other, and as soon as Joey saw her new friend, up went her crest and she said "Hello."

They were kept in separate cages side by side so that they could see and touch each other through the wires as it was thought safer not to put two strange birds together until they had become acquainted. (I might add here that this is a very wise precaution which should always be observed when two birds are first introduced.)

After about two weeks the birds seemed to be so friendly that they were allowed to live together in one cage, much to the delight of the family. During this time Joey was still friendly with her human family and continued to perform her few party pieces as usual. The mate also added a few words to the conversation as he did not want to be left out!

During the winter months the family built a breeding aviary complete with a stout wire flight and furnished with some rough branches and a brand new special type nesting box. Early in the following April on a bright sunny Sunday morning the birds were given their liberty in the aviary. They were delighted and flew and clambered about with crests erect calling to each other at the top of their voices. After an hour or two the first surge of excitement died down and the pair began to explore but did not take the slightest notice of the nesting box, much to everyone's disappointment.

It was not until the middle of May that Joey began to show interest in the nesting site. She spent all day climbing in and out, sometimes on her own and sometimes accompanied by her mate. Another week went by and then Joey suddenly disappeared and little was seen of her for the next few weeks. Some five weeks later faint squeakings were heard coming from the box. Joey's mate became very aggressive and objected to anyone's approaching the aviary except the father, who had always fed the pair.

Excitement ran high, and every available piece of literature that dealt with the breeding and feeding of cockatoos was read. It was decided to give the pair their usual mixed parrot food and their grit, cuttlebone and green food, together with some fresh fruit. In addition, a few cubes of whole-wheat bread that had been soaked in boiled milk were given daily and were eagerly eaten. As the squeaking became louder and more incessant it became clear that there were several chicks—and lusty ones too—in the nesting box. This was further borne out by the large quantities of food both parents consumed. The cock bird did quite a lot of the feeding both of the chicks and of his mate, and he was very busy all day long attending to the wants of his family.

The owners had no idea as to when the young would appear from inside the box and it was difficult to keep from having a look just to see, but nevertheless temptation was resisted. (It is always a wise thing, particularly in the case of a first nesting, to leave the birds entirely on their own and let nature take its normal course. Unwarranted interference may upset the pair, and a valuable nest of chicks can easily be lost. After

Hyacinthine macaw, ***Anodorhynchus hyacinthinus.***

Blue and yellow macaws, **Ara ararauna,** *with red and yellow macaws,* **Ara macao.** *Photo by H. V. Lacey.*

Blue and yellow macaw, **Ara ararauna.**

the first time, I think it permissible to take an occasional peep into the nesting box providing there is no unnecessary disturbance of the breeding pair.)

One morning about six weeks after the first squeakings were heard, the first young roseate cockatoo appeared on the top of the box alongside his father. He was a funny little creature with very short tail and wings and a lusty cry. The following day he was joined by another, and two days later two more appeared, to make the grand total of four healthy youngsters. It is easy to imagine the excitement in the family when they found the first chick that had left the box, but when three more were discovered their excitement really knew no bounds.

The parent birds were most attentive to their young for several weeks even though they could feed themselves quite well. Then came the problem of what to do with four baby cockatoos, particularly since nobody in the family wanted to part with them! It was finally reluctantly decided that it would be best for all concerned to send the four chicks to new homes so that other people could have the pleasure of a roseate cockatoo.

Great Black Cockatoo *(Probosciger atterrimus)*
Also known as the palm cockatoo and goliath cockatoo
Habitat: New Guinea, Australia

Only a picture can do justice to this ferocious-looking but good-natured creature. Those who know it well know that it is really quite gentle and playful, and very easily tamed. The fully grown adults are sometimes over 30 inches long, not counting the erectile crest. As the name indicates, the basic color is black with a somewhat greenish sheen, but the natural feather dust often makes the plumage appear more gray than black. Their crest is massive, the feathers spiny-looking; their eyes and huge beaks are black. They have bare areas on their cheeks that are somewhat wrinkled and may show a deep reddish flush which becomes more pronounced when the birds are angry or frightened. They are also said to stamp their feet when surprised.

Although these birds are striking in appearance, they are a little large for household pets. Nevertheless they make good exotic members of any aviary collection. Some have been trained to imitate the human voice, and their tone has been found to be clear and rich.

LORIES AND LORIKEETS
These make up a large group of nectar-feeding parrots from the

Australian and Indonesian area. Many are brilliantly colored. They vary considerably in size and are usually long-lived. Many will breed in captivity even in quite small aviaries. Because these species become so exceedingly tame and friendly, they are worth keeping even though their feeding habits require a little more care when they are kept as cage pets. Undoubtedly, they are seen to their best advantage when housed in aviaries. I cannot emphasize too strongly the need for strict hygiene in their food and water vessels and, of course, their general management.

Chattering Lory *(Lorius garrulus)*
Habitat: Indonesia

These interesting birds are about 12 inches. The sexes are similar in size and coloring. Their main color is deep crimson. The wings are green with yellow at the butts, the primaries are red and the under wing coverts are yellow. There is also a yellow band over the shoulders. The base of the tail is red turning to purple tinged with green. The bill is red.

These are not as free-breeders as the Swainson's lorikeet, although hybrids have been produced between the two species. Since they cannot stand intense cold, they require heat during the winter months. They make wonderful aviary birds and are excellent for show purposes.

Black-capped Lory *(Lorius lory)*
Habitat: New Guinea

This is an extremely beautiful species, with a stocky build and bold head; it is about 12 inches long. The top of the head is black, this color extending to the eyes and the nape of the neck. A band of red on the nape usually divides a deep black collar near the shoulders which again is often separated from the black shoulders by another red band. The wings are green with black shading on the ends of the flights. The mantle between them is bright red. The underparts are usually red and blue. The tail is blackish.

It will be seen from this description that it is a very colorful species, one well worth adding to a collection. I have no knowledge that they have as yet been bred in captivity, nor do I know their talking potential.

Scaly-breasted Lorikeet *(Trichoglossus chlorolepidotus)*
Habitat: Eastern Australia

Greene comments:

> It is a pity no better name could have been found for them than that by which they are generally known; for Scaly

Tui parakeet, **Brotogeris sanctithomae**. *Photo by T. Caravaglia.*

Red and yellow macaw, **Ara chloroptera.**

A pair of noble macaws, **Ara nobilis** *(female in full profile).*
Photo by L. van der Meid.

Chestnut-fronted macaw, **Ara severa.** *Photo by L. van der Meid.*

Lineolated parakeet, **Bolborhynchus lineola.** *Photo by H. Müller.*

Scaly-breasted lorikeet shown at four days old (above) and at one month (below). Photos by D. Thompson.

> Breast has a decidedly uncanny sound about it, reminding one of lizards and other creeping things the very reverse of attractive . . . elegance of figure, sprightliness of manner, and funny little ways during the season of love and courtship, these lorikeets are deserving of every commendation that can be bestowed upon them . . . it is to be expected that as they get to be better known they will become great favorites with amateurs generally.

The basic color is a vivid grass green. The wings are a darker green on their upper surface and bright red underneath. The breast is sprinkled with scale-like markings of a rich greenish yellow color. The beak is coral red, the legs and feet gray. Its size has been described as about half again as large as the budgerigar. The male and female are much alike, the female being a little smaller and more feminine in appearance.

Forsten's Lorikeet *(Trichoglossus haematodus forsteni)*

Habitat: Indonesia

These have color patterns much like their near relations the Swainson's and are at times mistaken for them by novice bird keepers. This bird seems to take well to captivity, and it quickly adapts. They breed well in quite small compartments. They soon become friendly with their owners and will allow themselves to be handled if care is taken not to frighten them. The back, wings and tail are a nice bright shade of green, paler at the nape. The head is purple with some blue, and there is also some bluish purple on the abdomen. The breast is reddish with dark bands. The overall length is about ten inches, which makes it a little smaller than the Swainson's.

Swainson's Lorikeet *(Trichoglossus haematodus moluccanus)*

Also known as blue mountain lorikeet or rainbow lorikeet

Habitat: Eastern Australia

These delightfully colored birds are some 12 inches in overall length, the sexes being similar in color. The head and throat are bluish purple, and the back, wings and tail are green, with a yellow band on the nape. The breast and under wing coverts are a beautiful vermilion red, and the underparts are bright blue. The tail coverts are yellow tipped with green, and the bill is orange red tipped with yellow.

Taken all in all they are a lovely blend of iridescent color, which is why they are often called rainbow lorikeets. They are most friendly and can be trained to come to hand on call. There are areas in Australia where wild flocks of these lorikeets come daily to feed from the hands of visitors—truly a wonderful sight!

When Swainson's (and all other lorikeets) are first acquired they must be kept in a warm, even temperature until they have become acclimated and used to their new way of feeding.

Ornate Lory *(Trichoglossus ornatus)*

Habitat: Celebes

These are mainly green lorikeets set off by areas of vivid red and blue that form a striking color pattern. Most of the head, including the areas around the eyes, is bright purplish blue, and the cheeks and throat are clear red. The chest and a patch on the neck are red with green at the tips; this gives a scale-like look which is most attractive. The sexes are colored the same.

Ornates are not widely kept, but they are seen occasionally in large collections. They are friendly little birds about ten inches long, three inches of which is tail. In aviaries large or small they are contented in-

Canary-winged parakeet, **Brotogeris versicolorus chiriri**. Photo by T. Caravaglia.

Bee bee parrot, **Brotogeris jugularis**. Photo by T. Caravaglia

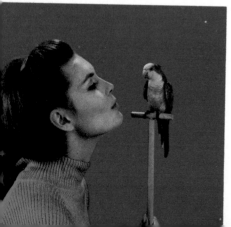

Quaker parakeet, **Myiopsitta monachus**. Photo by T. Caravaglia.

Blue-headed parrot,
***Pionus
menstruus***
*(male). Photo
courtesy of
Vogelpark
Walsrode.*

Hawk-headed parrot, **Deroptyus accipitrinus.** *Photo by T.
Caravaglia.*

mates, but they do not take as readily to life in a cage. They are good breeders and will nest quite readily if given the opportunity and a hollow log or nest box. They will also breed with other lorikeets.

PARROTS AND PARAKEETS

Green-winged King Parrot *(Alisterus chloropterus)*
Habitat: New Guinea

These are colored similarly to the Australian king parrot, but they are a few inches smaller. It is debatable which of these two species is the more handsome, but my personal opinion is that the king, because of its size, is the more commanding.

The beak is orange. The head, neck and breast are crimson red with rich deep blue from crown to back, the rump bright blue. The wings have a large brilliant pale green wing bar with dark flights, from which the bird derives its name.

The hen birds do not have the green wings. Their breast is a rusty green shade, and the back, neck and head are green.

Since all members of this group are commonly called king parrots, it is possible that green-wings have been bred in captivity but not recorded as such. It is known however that neither of these species is a very good breeder in aviaries, although a patient person should be able to get them to reproduce.

These birds are easy to feed, accepting fruits, berries and various green foods. They like to take baths, so facilities should be provided.

Australian King Parrot *(Alisterus scapularis)*
Habitat: Eastern Australia

These and their related species are generally considered to be the most richly colored of all the parrots. The average length is about 15 inches. King cocks are much more brilliant than their hens, making the sexes easy to distinguish. In the males the beak is orange red, dark at the tip and the head is bright red down to the shoulders on the upperside; the underside to the vent is a deep and richer red. The under tail coverts are black edged with wide bands of red. The tail itself is black. The wings and back are a bright clear green with a deep rich blue beginning on the lower back and shading into the black of the tail. A thin bluish collar follows the red of the neck, and there is a bright light green patch on the butts of the wings. The hens lack the green wing patches and are all green except for some red on the lower breast. The upper breast is olive green tinted with red, the upper tail is green and the rump blue. The beak is dark with a little orange shading.

Australian king parrots are spectacular birds which look their best when they are housed in large flighted aviaries. They have been known to breed in captivity, but whether or not they will attempt to do so is largely dependent on the individual pairs. The "grandfather clock" type of nest box should be used if a perpendicular hollow tree trunk about six feet high is not available.

The Duke of Bedford recommends a seed mixture of one part millet, one part oats, one part sunflower, one part hemp and one part peanuts along with fruit and green food. When they are feeding their young, an extra amount of sunflower seeds and peanuts should be offered.

Crimson-winged Parrot *(Aprosmictus erythropterus)*

Also known as red-winged parrot

Habitat: Australia and New Guinea

The crimson-winged is roughly the size of a pigeon—about 13½ inches. It derives its name from the large patch of deep crimson on each wing. The greater part of the plumage is rich grass-green; the back, shoulders and wing coverts are velvety black. The rump is blue; the eyes are reddish and the beak orange red. The female is less brilliantly colored; she has only a narrow strip of red on the wing and lacks the velvet-like black on the back.

The Duke of Bedford describes his crimson-wing as "a gorgeous ornament to the aviary" and goes on to say that "no living bird shows more striking contrasts of rich coloring, yet somehow there is nothing gaudy or crude about the whole combination."

The crimson-winged is a sturdy bird and breeds well in captivity. Experienced breeders report, however, that the male is inclined to be aggressive at breeding time. Greene states that the bird is "not very strong of beak, nor much given to whittling; consequently, a suitable nesting place must be provided for its accommodation, in the shape of a naturally or artificially hollowed log of wood, hung up in some quiet corner of the aviary."

New Caledonian Crested Parakeet *(Eunymphicus cornutus)*

Habitat: New Caledonia and Loyalty Islands

This species has two long black red-tipped feathers on the head forming a crest, but other than that it does not resemble the cockatoos or cockatiel. The forehead and crown are a red that fades to yellow at the back of neck and ear coverts, with the face sooty black. The rest of the plumage is green with blue on wings and tail. A few specimens have been maintained in captivity but I have no record of their having been bred or kept as cage birds.

*Celestial parrotlet, **Forpus coelestis**. Photo by L. van der Meid.*

*White-bellied caique, **Pionites leucogaster**. Photo by L. van der Meid.*

*Black-headed caique, **Pionites melanocephala**. Photo by H. Müller.*

Funereal cockatoo, **Calyptorhynchus funereus.** *In contrast to his solemn look and somber color, he makes a very engaging pet. Photo by L. van der Meid.*

White-crested cockatoo, **Cacatua alba,** *with sulphur-crested cockatoo,* **Cacatua galerita.**

"Budgies" are bred world-wide and countless varieties are bred for commercial distribution. Photo by H. V. Lacey.

Budgerigar *(Melopsittacus undulatus)*
Also known as undulated grass parakeet, shell parakeet or simply the parakeet

Habitat: Australia

No book on the parrot family of birds could be considered complete if it did not include the budgerigar, shortened affectionately to budgie. In America, when the one word "parakeet" is used ('keet for short) it refers to this species, although my readers know by now that there are literally dozens of varieties of parakeets. This particular one with the long scientific name is also known as the Australian shell parakeet, the zebra parakeet, the warbling grass parakeet and the canary parrot. For a long time it was mistakenly called a lovebird because of the affection displayed for each other by the pairs, but the term "lovebird" is more properly reserved for the stocky square-tailed African birds, which are much heavier bodied than the parakeet.

The descriptive names zebra, undulated and shell refer to the bird's distinctive markings: a zebra-striped or seashell pattern of black across its head, neck and wings. Budgerigar is an anglicization of the Australian bushmen's name for the bird, "betcherrygar," which can be roughly translated as "pretty good eating." It is pronounced *budg-er-ee-gar.*

While the original bird was green and yellow with black markings, because of scientific breeding it exists today in practically every color and combination of colors except red. (And rich indeed will become the first breeder to breed a red one.) In America, these parakeets have been divided into two general groupings, the normals and the rares. The normals come in four colors: green, blue-white, blue and chartreuse. All others are considered rares. Among these are the albinos (white with pink eyes), harlequins (white and blue, yellow and green with spotted markings on wings), lutinos (yellow with pink eyes), opalines (with narrower head stripings, wings the same ground color as the body and a lovely opalescent sheen) and yellow-faced blues (yellow coloring on the top of the head). It goes without saying that you will have to pay more for a rare than you will for a normal.

The budgerigar's diet is simple indeed. Everything is obtainable at pet shops: the correct mixture of seeds, the supplementary foods needed to provide additional vitamins and minerals, millet sprays, growing greens, gravel and cuttlebone.

The sections on training parrots and teaching them to talk are both applicable to budgerigars. Keep in mind that these are tiny birds and that their voices are tiny too. They do not sound like someone speaking in a room, but more like a voice coming over the telephone. It is a mistake to believe that only male budgerigars can learn to talk. This completely wrong assumption probably grew out of the fact that only the male canary sings. The female budgie can be taught to talk just as well as the male.

Among the chief reasons for the tremendous popularity of the budgie are the ease with which it can be bred and the fun of studying the laws of genetics by breeding birds in various color combinations.

Parakeets housed indoors are likely to breed at any time. However, spring and midwinter are the two most likely seasons. Obviously, making sure that you have a male and female is of first importance. Budgies do not vary in size and color, nor do they have any visible sexual organs. However, after the birds are about six months old, the sexes can be differentiated by the color of the cere—the swelling at the top of the bill around the nostrils. The male's cere is blue; the female's is tan or brownish. Until they are three months old the cere's color is nondescript.

Leadbeater's cockatoo, **Cacatua leadbeateri.**

Gang gang cockatoo,
Callocephalon
fimbriatum *(male).*
Photo courtesy of
San Diego Zoo.

Banksian red-tailed cockatoo, **Calyptorhynchus magnificus.** *Photo courtesy of San Diego Zoo.*

The age of the birds is important. A very young one can be recognized by the narrow black lines on the forehead. The baby starts to molt at about three months; these dark feathers are gradually replaced by light ones and the lines disappear. A male should be at least ten months old before it is bred and the female twelve. A healthy female will continue to breed for about five years and will raise two or even three nests a year, frequently laying a second round before the first fledglings have moved out. She will lay an egg every other day until five or six have been laid. They will begin to hatch in from 17 to 20 days, one bird at a time. It follows then that there will be fledglings of various ages in the nest at the same time. When hatched, the new birds are bare of feathers, and they remain that way for about a week.

Bourke's Parakeet *(Neophema bourkii)*

Habitat: Australia

Since this species of the grass parakeets breeds freely in captivity, it is frequently encountered. They are small birds of about the same size as an exhibition budgerigar but built on more generous lines. The sexes differ in color. The cock birds are brownish tinged with red above and darker on the rump and upper tail coverts. The head and back of the neck are daintily suffused with salmon red, and the forehead and eye stripe pale blue. The cheeks are rosy, with each feather edged in brown. The upper wing coverts and outer flights are violet blue, with the tail brownish tinged with blue. The hens are slighter in build and duller in color, with the blue frontal band practically absent.

They nest quite freely in large cages and small aviaries, making excellent and attentive parents. They are good birds for the beginner in parakeet breeding.

Scarlet-chested Parakeet *(Neophema splendida)*

Also known as the scarlet-breasted or splendid parakeet

Habitat: Southern Australia

The small but beautiful male bird is, quite literally, every color of the rainbow: red and orange breast, blue-violet head and wing coverts, green back and rump, yellow belly, and black bill. The female, as usual, is on the duller side. She has a plain green breast, and the blue on her forehead and cheeks is much paler. Her thighs and under tail coverts are yellow.

The scarlet-chested is one of the grass parakeets, so-called because they frequent the ground, feeding on grass and other seeds. Its voice is gentle and quite musical. The birds nest in a hollow limb and lay from three to five eggs, hatching them in about 18 days.

*A pair of turquoisine parakeets, **Neophema pulchella**. Like the budgerigar, this species is originally from Australis, but it is not yet as widely distributed and bred as the budgerigar. Photo by H. V. Lacey.*

Turquoisine Parakeet *(Neophema pulchella)*

Habitat: Southeastern Australia

Observers are agreed that the turquoisine, once considered almost extinct, is now being found in larger numbers, but it is still far from common. It does, however, breed well in captivity so chances are we will soon see more and more of turquoisines in pet shops and commercial aviaries.

In length it is about eight inches, which is the size of the exhibition budgerigar. The overall color is olive green; the forehead and face are

Great black cockatoo, **Probosciger aterrimus.** *Photo by Dr. H. R. Axelrod.*

216

Moluccan cockatoo, **Cacatua moluccensis**. *Photo by H. Müller.*

A pair of rose-breasted cockatoos, **Eulophus roseicapillus** *(male) with crest erect in profile. Photo by H. Müller.*

turquoise, and so are the wing bands. The male has a chestnut brown patch on the shoulder which the duller female frequently lacks. The underparts of the body are bright yellow, the long tapering tail bright green.

All who have kept turquoisines agree with Greene that they are, without exception, one of the most charming parakeets, combining the excellent qualities of "comeliness, hardihood, docility, and amiability." Their care and feeding are the same as the budgerigar's.

One ornithologist reports seeing wild turquoisines sticking leaves from the aromatic Australian tea-tree beneath their feathers, presumably to serve as a pesticide.

Rosella Parakeet *(Platycercus eximius)*
Also known as rose hill parakeet, eastern rosella parakeet and red rosella parakeet

Habitat: Australia

There are, in all, nine different broad-tailed parakeets grouped as

*Rosella parakeets **(Platycercus eximius)** are not only very colorful and easy to keep, but they also have pleasant voices or calls. Photo by H. V. Lacey.*

Yellow rosella parakeet
*(**Platycercus flaveolus**).*
Photo by H. V. Lacey.

rosellas, but when the one name "rosella" is used, it usually designates this species. The rosella makes a lovely aviary bird and, if properly kept, a good cage pet. Rosellas, if taken young, become quite attached to their owners. In most cases they are easy to train and teach a few words.

The head, neck and breast are bright scarlet, with the back blackish, broadly edged with yellow and greenish yellow. The rump is yellowish green. The cheeks carry a characteristic white patch which runs into red and greenish above. Their red plumage looks extremely handsome when they are flying in aviaries. A good pair will breed steadily for many years and raise their young well.

A rarer species is the smaller Stanley parakeet or western rosella *(Platycercus icterotis)*, which has yellow cheeks, with the head, neck and chest rich scarlet, and back markings similar to the eastern rosella. They breed freely in aviaries and are peace-loving birds. Other rosellas are the crimson *(Platycercus elegans)*, Adelaide *(P. adelaidae)*, the yellow or Murray *(P. flaveolus)*, the green or Tasmanian *(P. caledonicus)* and the mealy, blue or pale-headed *(P. adscitus)*. All of these birds are gracefully formed, and the majority have musical calls that make them particularly attractive.

Barnard's Parakeet *(Platycercus barnardi)*
Also known as mallee ringneck
Habitat: Eastern Australia

This beautiful broad-tail is named after a famous 18th century French naturalist. Its distinguishing mark is a band of deep red that stretches across the forehead from eye to eye. The rest of the head and most of the body are shaded a delicate pastel green. It has a yellow ring around its neck and a mantle that is rich deep blackish blue. The wings are of a

Scaly-breasted lorikeet, **Trichoglossus chlorolepidotus**. Photo by Irene and Michael Morcombe.

*Opposite: Chattering lory, **Lorius garrulus**. Photo by Dr. H. R. Axelrod.*

221

darker blue-green, and the flight feathers are a blackish blue. There is a patch of pale yellow on the lower breast, and the tail is dark green turning blue at the sides and tip. The beak is bluish. The overall length is 13 inches. The female's beak and head are smaller, and she is usually duller than the male. The young show almost no difference in color. It is hard to distinguish the sexes, as one can only judge by head size. When a year old, the young molt and it is then that their adult color develops.

Unlike most parrots, this beautiful bird has a somewhat pleasing voice and a call that resembles "Twink-wink-wink . . ."

Most authorities agree that while the Barnard has occasionally been bred in captivity it is not an easy thing to do, so this should serve as a challenge to anyone wanting to attempt it. Perhaps in the right circumstances with the right matched pair success will be achieved.

Port Lincoln Parrot *(Platycercus zonarius)*
Also known as yellow-naped parakeet or twenty-eight parrot
Habitat: Southwestern Australia

I can do no better than to quote W.T. Greene:

> It is a handsome bird. The forehead is crossed by a narrow crimson band; the head is blackish brown, changing gradually into blue on the cheeks; a band of bright yellow encircles the back of the neck; the upper surface generally is of a deep grass green color, which becomes paler towards the shoulders; the primaries and spurious wing feathers are blackish brown, but the external web of each feather is deep blue; the two central feathers of the tail are very deep grass green, but the next pair on either side passing to blue, and are terminated by bluish white tips; the rest of the tail feathers are green at the base passing into blue, and ending with white; the chest is dark green, and the rest of the undersurface is a paler shade of the same color; the irides are dark brown; the bill horn color; and the legs and feet dark brown.
>
> The Yellow Naped Parakeet is a native of Western Australia, where John Gould found it very abundant in the vicinity of Swan River. It is hardy, and frequently caged by the Australians, who call it the Twenty Eight Parrot, from the fancied resemblance of the last two syllables of its call note to those words. Although essentially a ground bird, it breeds in the hollow limbs of trees, making no nest, but laying its seven or nine white eggs on the semi-decayed wood.

There are generally two broods in the season, which extends from October to January.

It has not so far distinguished itself very prominently as a talker, but it has a melodious voice for a Parakeet, and learns to whistle an air with facility and correctness. Being of a gentle but withal not timid nature, it soon becomes very familiar, not only with the person who feeds it, but with the other inmates of the house whom it usually recognizes by a repetition of its peculiar cry.

There is very little outward difference between the sexes; but the adult female is decidedly smaller than her mate, and the colors of her plumage are duller.

The young resemble their parents from the first, but are considerably smaller, when they leave the nest.

Queen Alexandra's Parakeet *(Polytelis alexandrae)*

Also known as princess parrot or Princess of Wales parakeet

Habitat: Western Australia

This rare species was named by John Gould in honor of the Princess of Wales, later Queen Alexandra of England. It should not be confused with the Alexandrine ring-neck. Queen Alexandra's parakeets are one of the largest of the Australians, being some 17 inches overall with most of their length given over to a magnificent tail.

Free breeders in captivity, they make a beautiful display in an aviary. Docile by nature, their call is quite pleasant.

The top of the head is pale blue with the throat and cheeks a rosy pink; the nape and back are an olive green which fades into the rump as a bluish olive. The thighs are red and the breast grayish dull green. The tail, which is so outstanding, has a definite rosy color all through. The hen birds are more slaty in color and are not quite as large as their male counterparts. Immature young are similar to the hens. A blue mutation has been reported.

Barraband's Parakeet *(Polytelis swainsonii)*

Also known as superb parakeet

Habitat: Southeastern Australia

Barraband's parakeet (named after a French painter who specialized in birds) is readily identified by the shield of deep scarlet which hangs like a crescent moon below its throat. The overall color is a rich deep green, while the forehead, cheeks and throat are lemon-yellow. The flight feathers of the wings are blue. The beak is dull red, the legs black. The length is about 15 inches, eight of which are tail. The female is plain green, lacking both the yellow crown and throat and the scarlet

*Crimson-winged parrot **Aprosmictus erythropterus**. Photo by H. Müller.*

*Black-capped lory, **Lorius lory** and chattering lory, **Lorius garrulus** (head in profile). Photo by H. Müller.*

crescent. She does, however, retain the blue on the wings. So different are the sexes that for years—particularly since the males flock together during the nesting season—they were thought to be two different species.

Among Barraband fanciers, there seems to be a difference of opinion regarding their congeniality with other birds. It appears to vary with the individual. They are hardy and long-lived birds and adapt themselves quickly to the northern climate. While they are mainly seed-eaters, they do in the wild feed also on nectar, so the diet recommended for nectar-feeding birds, as well as mealworms, should be given to them at regular intervals.

Red Shining Parakeet (Prosopeia tabuensis splendens)
Habitat: Fiji Islands

As their name indicates, the plumage of these parrots has a metallic sheen. Their head, neck and underparts are a beautiful shining clear crimson red with the nape of the neck a bright blue; the back and rump are green.

They are large birds some 18 inches in overall length, and the few specimens that have been kept as pets have proved most satisfactory, becoming very tame and learning an occasional word. They feed on the usual parrot seed mixture but need more than the usual quantity of fresh food and green food to keep them fit and their plumage glossy.

Red-rumped Parakeet (Psephotus haematonotus)
Also known as blood-rumped parakeet or red-backed parakeet
Habitat: Australia

With the exception of the budgerigar the red-rumped parakeet is the most widely kept of the Australian parakeets. The male's plumage is a rich grass green with a bluish cast in certain lights, especially on the head and face where it is velvet-like. The belly is yellow fading into white at the vent, the rump is bright blood red, the shoulders are blue and the tail is dark bluish green. The beak is dark horn, the legs and feet gray.

In addition to being easy breeders, red-rumps have a very soft musical call which is quite pleasant. Young males taken in hand at an early age become most endearing pets and learn to repeat a few words. They do better if not confined in close quarters with other species.

W.T. Greene has this to say about red-rumps in his book *Parrots in Captivity:*

> Its general disposition, at least as far as our experience of
> the species goes, is exceedingly unamiable, and we cannot

A pair of scarlet-chested parakeets, **Neophema splendida** *(male with blue head and red throat). Photo by H. Müller.*

Budgerigar, **Melopsittacus undulatus** *(female with babies). Photo by H. V. Lacey.*

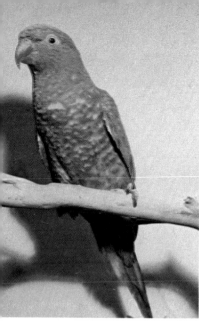

Scaly-breasted lorikeet,
***Trichoglossus
chlorolepidotus.***

Ornate lory, ***Trichoglossus
ornatus.*** *Photo by H. V. Lacey.*

Swainson's lorikeet, ***Trichoglossus
haematodus moluccanus.***

Australian king parrot,
Alisterus scapularis. *Photo
by H. Müller.*

Shown is a hybrid from a cross between a female red-rumped parakeet **(Psephotus haematonotus)** *and a male green rosella* **(Platycercus caledonicus)**.

recommend its being kept with other Parakeets; a pair, however, placed in a roomy aviary by themselves, will very soon set about reproducing their species, and succeed to admiration, which as the bird is handsome, extremely lively, hardy, and gifted with quite a musical voice, is a fact to be remembered.

The female is greyish green with a mottled appearance, arising from the fact of each feather being margined with a narrow line of a deeper shade of the general color of the plumage; the shoulders are blue, the tail has a deep shade of blue, and the rump is bright green. So dissimilar are the sexes in appearance that they have been taken for different species by some of the earlier writers on Australian Parakeets.

These birds breed as freely in captivity as the Budgerigar or the Cockatiel, laying from three to five smaller eggs which the female alone incubates, her mate rendering her no assistance, his cheerful song, as he sits at no great distance from the hollow log that contains the precious eggs, excepted; for he does not even feed her, nor, as far as we have been able to ascertain, does he feed the young until these have left their natal log, and are able to fly about after him, and importune him for food.

We have found that half a cocoanut husk cemented into a small box made a capital nest that was much appreciated by these birds, which do not seem to care about excavating a dwelling for themselves, when a ready-made one has been placed at their disposal.

"There are no song birds in Australia" is one complaint, more or less founded on fact, one often hears; but the Red Rump sings, actually sings a very passable song, a fact which has procured for him in Germany the name of *Singsittich*.

There is a yellow form of the Red Rump which is much more pallid, and although the birds do not show clear yellow throughout, there is considerably more yellow in their plumage. It has been reported that odd birds with broken or pied plumage have been bred, but I do not know of any strain that has been established. Without a doubt red-rumps are an ideal species for the novice who wants to start parakeet breeding.

Many-colored Parakeet *(Psephotus varius)*
Also known as mulga parrot

Note the brown patch on the shoulder of this turquoisine parakeet cock. Photo courtesy of San Diego Zoo.

Barnard's parakeet, **Platycercus bar-nardi**. *Photo by H. Müller.*

Turquoisine parakeet, **Neophema pulchella**.

Habitat: Australia

The many-color is a beautiful bird that lives up to its name. With the advances of aviculture it has become more and more popular; at one time it was considered difficult to keep because it was susceptible to septicemia. Modern antibiotics have lessened this danger.

The head and shoulders are greenish blue, with the forehead, wing and under tail coverts bright yellow. The nape of the neck is deep red, with the thighs and underparts orange. Many-colors breed well in captivity and, although they are slightly smaller, will interbreed with red-rumps.

Hooded Parakeet *(Psephotus dissimilis)*

Habitat: Northern Australia

This 12-inch bird is frequently mistaken for the golden-shouldered parakeet, a much rarer species. It has a black hood and a long broad yellow wing patch. The upper part of the wing is a sooty gray. The sides of neck, throat, breast and part of the rump are cobalt blue. The under tail coverts are orange-salmon. The tail is blackish bronze-green.

In the wild, it burrows into the nests of termites, where it hollows out a chamber and lays its eggs. In captivity, it thrives better in an aviary than as a cage bird.

The Duke of Bedford describes the hooded as "a glorious creature, the male, with his big yellow wing patches and graceful dancing flight, looking like some enormous butterfly."

Red-capped Parakeet *(Purpureicephalus spurius)*

Also known as pileated parakeet

Habitat: Southwestern Australia

Both males and females possess green backs and wings and purple breasts, which are highlighted by a ruby-red cap. This in turn is complemented by the golden green cheeks and the gray-blue feathers under the surface of the tail. The coloring is almost iridescent, the hues changing with the light. The primary difference between the sexes is the dull red shade on the rump of the male, in contrast to the yellowish green on the female. The overall length of both sexes is generally 16 inches.

Especially appreciated are the gentle lovable disposition of the bird, its inoffensive habits and the softness and sweetness of its notes sung in low tones. Being extremely social and gentle, they may safely be housed even with the tiniest birds.

Red-cheeked Parrot *(Geoffroyus geoffroyi)*

Habitat: Australia, New Guinea, Indonesia

This somewhat scarce medium size parrot comprises some 16

subspecies which vary in the arrangement of their color pattern according to the area from which they come. Many live on islands, and their restricted breeding accounts for these many local variations. Their diet consists of the various fruits and berries that grow with such profusion in the tropics. I feel that it is their feeding habits which keep them from being in greater demand since they are such attractive birds.

There is quite a difference in the coloring of the two sexes, with the males being the most brightly colored. The basic color is bright green with a red suffusion on the front of the head, cheeks and throat, while the top of the head is a rich blue suffused with violet. The beak is red and tipped with bright orange in the cocks, whereas the hens' beaks are black. The tail is short. The head of the hen is dull brownish, and her general coloring is less brilliant than the cock's.

They appear to tame quite readily, but I have no information as to their talking ability nor do I know if they have ever been bred in captivity.

Singing Parrot *(Geoffroyus heteroclitus)*
Habitat: Solomons, New Britain, New Ireland

This bird is related to the red-cheeked parrot and like it lives on islands. It is quite rare in captivity but is worthy of mention because of its distinctive singing parrot call which is quite different from the more commonly known, harsher call notes.

Their general color is green with the head a dull yellow terminating in a light blue gray around the neck. The undersides of the wings are blue and the beak yellow. In the hen the beak is black and the yellow on the head is replaced by blue gray. The undersides of the wings are not as bright blue as those of the cock birds.

Because of their rarity, little is known of their behavior in captivity, but some observers state that they are of a somewhat timid disposition.

Grand Eclectus *(Eclectus roratus)*
Habitat: New Guinea, adjacent islands, extreme northern Australia

These birds are among the most vividly colored of all parrots, which is probably why they were worshipped at one time by the natives. The grand eclectus certainly lives up to its name in color. In addition, the sexes are entirely different in coloring, which makes them easy to distinguish at all times. The cock birds are bright rich green on the top parts, shading lighter toward the head, with red patches on the sides of the breast. The under wing coverts are also red. The top side of the tail is greenish with blue and white ends, and the underside is bluish black with yellow ends. Another striking feature is that the lower part of the

*A pair of eastern rosellas, **Platycercus eximius** (male, rear). Photo by H. V. Lacey.*

*Western rosella, **Platycercus icterotis**. Photo by H. Müller.*

A pair of mealy rosellas, **Platycercus adscitus** *(male facing front).*
Photo by H. Müller.

A pair of crimson rosellas, **Platycercus elegans** *(male body in full pro-*
file). Photo by H. Müller.

A grand eclectus parrot **(Eclectus roratus)** *being stick trained by a professional bird handler. Photo by K. Donnelly.*

beak is black and the upper part is yellowish shading into orange pink at the base. The hen birds are much more brightly colored, with black beaks, an intense red head and breast, a blue collar on the nape of the neck and a blue belly set off by deep maroon on the wings. The undersides are shaded with blue, maroon and green, which shades into the black of the flight feathers. The vent area is red, and the upper side of the tail is maroon, shading to orange at the ends. The feathers of both sexes have an unusual appearance, like fur that has been combed, which is quite uncommon among parrots.

When given the freedom of a medium sized aviary, they will go to nest and rear youngsters if they are left to themselves and the nest is not disturbed. There are many subspecies, all brightly colored with the same differences in color patterns between the sexes. Unfortunately, very few are imported.

Pigmy Parrots *(Micropsitta* species)

Habitat: New Guinea and adjacent islands, Solomons

These extremely tiny members of the parrot family are only about three to four inches long. Their color is mainly green, paler on the underparts; the front of the head is a dull yellow shade. The tail coverts are yellow, the underside of the tail black and yellow, and the beak horn colored. Some species have blue on the head and red on the belly. Few captured specimens have lived long because their feeding habits are poorly known. Some twenty species and subspecies of the little birds have been recorded in New Guinea and the surrounding islands. These are quite the smallest of all the parrots, and it is a great pity that we are not as yet able to see them in our part of the world.

Racket-tailed Parrot *(Prioniturus platurus)*

Habitat: Celebes and adjacent Indonesian islands

This is an unusual looking species some 13 inches overall, including the unique tail. Their main color is green, while the lower part of the neck is a pastel lavender with a pink patch above. Beneath the wing coverts, which range from gray to lilac, are areas of rich golden yellow. The tails are dark with two very long central feathers extending out, but without the usual webbing except at the far ends, which are racket-shaped. These strange-looking tail feathers give the birds their name. The few specimens in captivity are kept as show pieces. No attempts have been made to breed them. The hen birds are not so bright in color and their racket-shaped tail feathers are shorter. Nothing is known of the bird's talking potential.

Blue-naped Parrot *(Tanygnathus lucionensis)*

Habitat: Philippines and adjacent islands to the south

These birds are mainly green with slender bodies and long tails. They are extremely popular as pets in their native country, although not too many find their way to the United States or Europe. Their size, including the long broad tail which makes up about a third of their total length, is from 12 to 14 inches. Their beaks are quite large, red with a yellow tip, and the lower mandible is solid yellow. The top of the head is bright blue; the wings are variegated with blue, and some have bright yellow edges. They become very tame, are easy to handle and can be taught many tricks.

Great-billed Parrot *(Tanygnathus megalorynchos)*

Habitat: Eastern Indonesian islands and islands east of the Celebes

These birds have the largest beaks of the genus and, in fact, of the majority of the parrot family; for this reason alone they are outstanding. Fairly large birds, they are about 17 inches overall. There are eight subspecies. The huge beaks are bright coral red, the eyes yellow. Their overall color is a pleasing shade of blue-green. The smaller wing coverts are a blue-black edged with yellow, the larger wing coverts bluish green.

Queen Alexandra's parakeet, **Polytelis alexandrae.** Photo by H. V. Lacey.

Barraband parakeet, **Polytelis swainsonii.** Photo by H. V. Lacey.

Three grand eclectus parrots, **Eclectus roratus,** under the care of a native of Papua New Guinea. The red female is very distinct. Photo by G. R. Allen.

This photo illustrates why the Port Lincoln parrot, **Platycercus zonarius,** is also called the yellow-naped parakeet. Photo by F. Prenzel.

The somewhat short tail is a greenish yellow, and there is a bright blue patch on the rump. In the hens the black and blue on their wings is replaced by green. In spite of their rather fearsome beaks, most specimens are surprisingly gentle.

Cockatiel *(Nymphicus hollandicus)*

Also known as Quarrion

Habitat: Australia

These fascinating little birds are the only members of their genus. While somewhat more somber than the other Australian parakeets, they have many fetching ways which endear them to their owners. After the budgerigar and canary, the cockatiel is probably the world's favorite cage and aviary bird.

The cock birds are a soft shade of dove gray, with the face, throat and cheek areas yellowish. The ear coverts are an orange-red which deepens

A trio of healthy cockatiels in a bird dealer's shop. Several varieties, other than the normal gray or wild form, are now bred commercially. Photo by V. Serbin.

with age. Their outstanding feature is the upright gray crest with a yellow base. The hens and young ones are duller than the adult cocks, lack the orange-red ear coverts and have barred outer tail feathers. As juvenile males mature and molt, the outer tail feathers are replaced with feathers that are gray with some yellow. Single birds, both cocks and hens, become extremely tame and friendly and can soon be allowed the freedom of the house. In fact, some grow so tame that they can be allowed to fly free like pigeons. Although there is a difference of opinion about their vocabulary—some claiming that it is limited, others thinking them to be fine talkers—they do have a clear voice and a natural, musical call.

Many cockatiels form strange friendships with other household pets and give their owners a great deal of pleasure with their playful antics. Their care is the same as for budgerigars, and their simple diet is based on canary seed, a little millet, and sunflower seeds. They are partial to green foods, and some will eat fruit.

Cockatiels are now completely domesticated. In addition to the normal birds, albino, pied and lutino varieties are available.

NEW ZEALAND ODDITIES

It will, I know, be fully realized that there are many other members of the parrot family that could not possibly be dealt with in a book of this scope. However, there are two more species, both from New Zealand, that I would like to mention here.

Owl Parrot *(Strigops habroptilus)*

These are strange members of the parrot family that fly mostly at night and whose habits are more like the owls' than the parrots'. In their native land they are also called the kakapo. At one time their feathers were used to decorate native garments, which has undoubtedly contributed to their rarity. They are short, thick parrots with small hooked bills and are mainly green in color. They spend much of their time on the ground and live on fruits, seeds and roots.

Kea *(Nestor notabilis)*

These parrots and their way of life are surrounded in mystery. They live in very rough, mountainous country where they have been accused of killing sheep. This, I think, is only hearsay; most probably the birds were seen eating the fat from the backs of sheep dead from other causes. Their color is dark green with reddish brown markings. Their bills are rather unusual, being long and curved, undoubtedly useful for digging out the roots and grubs that form their diet. These strange birds tame quite well and have, in fact, actually been bred in several zoos.

Red-rumped parakeet, **Psephotus haematonotus** *(female). Photo by H. Müller.*

Many-colored parakeet, **Psephotus varius**. *Photo by K. Hindwood.*

*Right: Hooded parrot, **Psephotus dissimilis**. Photo by A. Clements.*

Below: Male hooded parrot (with black cap) and female. Photo by L. Robinson.

243

For the camera or exhibition only those specimens in perfect plumage and proper training are selected first. Shown is a rosella parakeet photographed by H. V. Lacey.

Exhibiting

The exhibiting of parrots is gradually increasing all over the world. Most people know budgerigars as exhibition birds, since many thousands of them are shown and admired every year. Some of the smaller species such as lovebirds, conures and Australian parakeets are also easy to show because of their convenient size. The larger specimens—macaws, cockatoos and the larger amazons—present more of a problem because of the large cages they require. In spite of this, many enthusiastic owners travel long distances to show their spectacular birds.

One has only to go to an exhibition of cage birds to see the general public flocking around the parrot section even when only a few commonplace species are being shown. There is always something fascinating about the parrot family, particularly when they condescend to talk in public.

Birds sent to an exhibition should always be in perfect feather with all toes and claws complete, and they should, of course, be good examples of their species. The smaller breeds are sometimes exhibited in true pairs, a cock and hen, but the larger ones, although occasionally shown in pairs, are mostly singles. Lovebirds and the smaller parakeets are exhibited in box-type show cages. Macaws, cockatoos and the large parrots and parakeets are shown in their every day cage or on a stand.

The household pet requires no special training for exhibitions, but those kept in aviaries need to become accustomed to a show cage and to sit correctly on the perches. If the birds are not trained in this respect the judges cannot ascertain their full value. Many times when judging these birds I have been grieved not to be able to give really fine birds their full due because they just would not allow me to see them properly. Many of them scrambled in corners, presenting only their rumps to view. Any time spent in training birds to behave correctly in a show cage is well worthwhile, always paying dividends in the end.

It is reasonably easy to get the smaller birds to show themselves off in a show cage. My method is to house the birds some time prior to an exhibition in a large stock cage and then hang an old show cage over an open door, enticing the birds to go into it by means of a tidbit. It is surprising how quickly the vast majority of these birds settle down in a show cage. They are then kept in an area with a good deal of pedestrian traffic to accustom them to the idea of strangers approaching.

The travelers should be given their usual food when sent to a show, and an ample supply of the same mixture should be included in the traveling box. The lories and other nectar-feeding birds will, of course, need their own special diet. I have found that these species take readily to cages and that they make exceptionally colorful exhibits.

Great-billed parrot,
**Tanygnathus
megalorynchos.**

Red-capped parakeet, **Purpureicephalus spurius.** *Photo by H. Müller.*

Cockatiel, **Nymphicus hollandicus** *(male). Photo by H. V. Lacey.*

Index

Page numbers printed in *italics* refer to illustrations or photographs.

Owl parrot, **Strigops habroptilus.** *Photo by P. Leysen.*

Opposite: Kea parrot, **Nestor notabilis.** *Photo by Dr. H. R. Axelrod.*